SO, WHAT'S THE BOTTOM LINE?

SO, WHAT'S THE BOTTOM LINE?

76 **Proven Marketing Tips & Techniques**
for building your business
and personal brand

Yitzchok Saftlas

SO, WHAT'S THE BOTTOM LINE?

Proven Marketing Tips & Techniques *for* building your business and personal brand

Published in New York, New York, by Morgan James Publishing. Morgan James and The Entrepreneurial Publisher are trademarks of Morgan James, LLC.
www.MorganJamesPublishing.com

The Morgan James Speakers Group can bring authors to your live event. For more information or to book an event visit The Morgan James Speakers Group at
www.TheMorganJamesSpeakersGroup.com.

A **free** eBook edition is available with the purchase of this print book.

ISBN 978-1-63047-524-6 paperback
ISBN 978-1-63047-526-0 eBook
ISBN 978-1-63047-525-3 hardcover
Library of Congress Control Number:
2014922134

CLEARLY PRINT YOUR NAME ABOVE IN UPPER CASE

Instructions to claim your free eBook edition:
1. Download the Shelfie app for Android or iOS
2. Write your name in **UPPER CASE** above
3. Use the Shelfie app to submit a photo
4. Download your eBook to any device

In an effort to support local communities and raise awareness and funds, Morgan James Publishing donates a percentage of all book sales for the life of each book to Habitat for Humanity Peninsula and Greater Williamsburg.

Get involved today, visit
www.MorganJamesBuilds.com

Habitat for Humanity
Peninsula and
Greater Williamsburg
Building Partner

CONTENTS

SECTION I: BUSINESS STRATEGIES FOR SUCCESS — P.1

Thou Shalt be Prepared — P.2

A true professional is always equipped with the tools of his trade to spring into action at a moment's notice. In addition to making a positive impression, preparation sets you apart from the competition and can help get your name in the public eye.

Greatly Appreciated — P.5

The power of a simple thank you in the business world can send your stock soaring to new heights. Just keep saying thank you...and watch the results!

The Times Demand Urgency — P.7

Undue pressure, without a cause or a goal, is worth avoiding, but pressure born from urgency and ambition can be a positive and driving force of energy for your organization. Beat your deadlines, but don't let your deadlines beat you.

Geared Up & Ready to Go — P.9

Expecting the unexpected sounds like an oxymoron, but there is more than one good reason to devote time and energy to planning for contingencies. Leap ahead in response to unfolding events, rather than letting them throw you for a loss.

Marketing Aside... Some Gratitude — P.12

Offering thanks to those who have given of themselves and their resources is one of the most basic forms of humanity. And yes, even a form of advertising as well.

"QPR" — P.14

Whether your company features a product or service, be sure to position and market it properly to command the appropriate price model and fee structure.

Listen & Learn — P.16

We all know the famous saying, "Humans were created with two ears and one mouth." It takes self-discipline to choose to listen, rather than to speak. However, many have perfected the art. Learn to be an effective listener and observe the impact on your professional growth.

V

Curing Toyota's Woes with Tylenol? — P.38

How would Toyota salvage their longtime brand-image of trustworthiness, consistency and reliability, and successfully guide their company through a damaging public relations fiasco? When doing "damage control," truthful consistent communication coupled with a proactive plan is the best public relations marketing strategy.

The 11 "Power Words" of Marketing — P.41

When you are communicating to your customers, choose words wisely – the right words can make all the difference in the world.

Push the Envelope — P.45

Thanks to the advantages offered by direct-mail, thousands of organizations have been able to keep donors informed and generate contributions year after year. When you are communicating to your customers via mail, be sure to choose your words wisely.

3 Cardinal Rules for Direct Mail Marketing — P.48

Raising money for non-profit organizations is always tough. In tough economic times, non-profits are forced to review and reevaluate their fundraising strategies even more. A few general, simple and practical tips that can be applied to any organization's fundraising techniques – during good times and bad.

Effective Teasers, Headlines, and Book Titles — P.51

Make sure the message you are conveying in your communications are clear, accurate and detailed.

Four Golden Rules for Powerful Headlines! — P.54

Henry S. Levy had a problem. The Brooklyn baker was having a difficult time selling his line of freshly baked rye bread products. Mr. Levy knew that a powerful message that would grab people's attention, get them reading, talking and buying, had to be delivered to the public.

SECTION III: OUT OF THE BOX MARKETING – P.57

Be Different! — P.58

I'm often posed the same question: "What is one of the most important factors for launching a successful marketing campaign?" My answer: "Don't be afraid of being different!"

Smelling the Money! — P.60

Come up with a creative marketing scheme that will net your company publicity and profits.

A Behind the Scenes Look at Political Marketing — P.172

It's the same every year. November rolls around and millions of Americans turn out on Election Day to vote in the elections. You know what that means — massive political advertising campaigns. Create a political campaign strategy designed to touch the heart and soul of the voters.

3 Tricks in Getting Free Publicity — P.176

How does a business get its message out to the public? By being proactive in its approach to marketing. Use every creative avenue to get your product and message across.

Fundraising by the Book — P.180

Remembering special events is not only important for marital harmony, it also can bring payoffs for something else near and dear to your heart – your non-profit organization. Learn how to attain new fundraising records from your milestone events.

A Lesson in Marketing from the Feds — P.182

Not all of us are blessed to sell bread or ice cream that everyone feels compelled to buy. A look at how to make your job easier by placing your customers in the driver's seat and making their priorities, yours.

SECTION VII: SUSTAINING YOUR BUSINESS (CUSTOMER RETENTION) – P.185

Understanding Customer Retention — P.186

You are the proud owner of a thriving business with lots of customers. Like every other entrepreneur, you want to continue increasing your sales and profits. Start writing a personal thank you note to your #1 client, today!

"Customer Retention" Tips & Techniques — P.190

A common misconception is that customer retention tactics are only for certain entities doing lots of repeat business, such as supermarkets and restaurants. Is that so? A close examination of the situation.

"Customer Retention" Case Studies — P.193

They say that it's difficult to understand somebody else until you've been in their shoes. When it comes to improving customer retention, try standing in the footwear of the trendsetting online shoe store, Zappos.com.

"Customer Retention" Loyalty Programs — P.196

When it comes to aviation firsts during the year of 1981, most history books focus on the creation of the famous Boeing 767 jetliner and how it helped revolutionize modern air travel. But very few mention a feat that helped revolutionize the overall airline industry from a marketing perspective.

Failure is Not an Option! — P.228

For those old enough to remember things such as record players, telegrams and rotary telephones, the story of Apollo 13 will probably ring a bell. Learn to avoid failure by capitalizing on unique opportunities for the future.

Turning Over a New Leaf — P.231

Even in a bad economy, someone with an entrepreneurial mindset remains optimistic. Some creative ideas to get you into an entrepreneurial mindset and get your business in shape for the future.

Lessons From a Renovated Bathroom — P.233

Do it yourself home improvement projects and the marketing industry have a great deal in common; they both require proper planning. Both need the proper materials, a well researched plan, and the time to finish the project.

Brochures Help You Close the Deal (Make Sure You Have Them in Time) — P.236

Did you ever find yourself being asked in the middle of a presentation if you have anything in writing? Anything that's put into writing and presented attractively should be impressive enough to assist in closing any deal.

Focus Day: Here to Stay — P.239

Revenue-generating activities comprise the lifeblood of any business. However, we often allow any number of distractions to draw us away from these truly vital tasks. That's why we must learn to discipline ourselves to truly sharpen our focus.

FORWARD

by the Honorable Robert L. Turner,
U.S. Congressman and Noted Media Executive

My first job in advertising involved the placing of brand commercials into network TV programs. It seemed simple enough. All one had to do was match the audience characteristics with the customer profile of the brand. I was employed by Bristol Myers, one of the largest advertisers in network television.

Bristol would buy dozens of TV spots every week in numerous programs for about 20 brands. The networks would sell the time in packages over a calendar quarter and the packages of commercial time would consist of highly coveted spots like M*A*S*H or "Bewitched" and other programs of lesser value.

Each brand manager wanted the best programs available for their brand and tended to be somewhat unreasonable when their brands were placed in the bottom end of the packages. It did not take me long to figure out that there was not enough top end programs to satisfy the demands of some 20 very narrowly focused brand managers. The solution was to buy all high-end programs but the cost advantage to the packages was substantial enough to make that approach impractical. The answer was to simply allocate the brand positions as fairly as possible and apply a measure of diplomacy in dealing with brand management.

The critical starting point to the process was to thoroughly know the objectives of each brand as well as the audience characteristics of each program. Compromises would be made but the compromiser had to understand the relative value of each component before a decision was made. Demographic and psychographic statistics were studied and reviewed, rating trends were analyzed and cost comparisons and competitive data were worked over until the late hours.

Some years later, I was lured away from Bristol Myers for a position at CBS. At that time I was Director of Advertising Services for US and

Canada and responsible for over $100,000,000 in measured media expenditures, as well as running an in-house ad agency and a syndicated TV program division.

The CBS job put me on a different career path from my roots in advertising but I came to see that all the principles and truism I learned in advertising were applicable in every aspect of my business experience and even extended into my late career in politics.

As I read and then re-read **SO, WHAT'S THE BOTTOM LINE?,** my mind was flooded with each chapter by memories of many successful efforts but more often of failed attempts. The hits soon get taken for granted but the misses stay with you. My business was one of high risks and high reward. It is the nature of independent television production and distribution and it is a business that is highly competitive and ever changing. Not unlike every other business.

Each business large or small must convince a customer, client, consumer, investor or the general public of the unique qualities your product or service has to offer. The success/failure rate is often determined by the message and how it is delivered. A good product or a great idea may never see the light of day if the message is poorly presented or improperly delivered.

What Yitzchok Saftlas has done is design a compass to guide the experienced executive or the marketing novice through any step in planning or organizing a selling strategy. His book is a check list to compare any plan with the ideal. As I said, compromises will be made but one should start with the ideal and evaluate the relative benefits of deviation.

As I was going through each chapter, I compared my actual experience with certain campaigns and presentations against the truisms in the book. From memory, I measured the effectiveness of these in the real world versus a projected outcome if the ideal had been implemented. It is clear to me that the time to read this book is before and during the planning stage.

The wise will read the appropriate verses before any plan is presented. This is a book to read and then put in your desk for easy reference.

PREFACE

How this book came to be...

Tap into any business conversation today, and at some point you'll hear the words uttered, "So what's the bottom line?" Perhaps you'll hear, "The bottom line is..." or another comment where "the bottom line" is mentioned. In most cases, it refers to the monetary value that something is projected to cost. However, another primary reason that it's mentioned is in order to keep focus on a no-nonsense solution to the challenge at hand.

Most executives are constantly challenging themselves in the course of their career in their quest to apply their experiences to further their company's mission and goals. The best among them continue to learn and are committed to inner growth. But there is one thing that all successful executives have in common: they know how to cut through complex challenges and get straight to "the bottom line."

I feel that I can relate to this because in my entire business experience, I've been on the lookout for opportunities to gain insight. Some of the lessons I have gained in the course of my career may seem basic; many were radical, but all were cutting edge at the moment.

But my favorite lessons were always the ones I've learned from people whom I've come in contact with. People have always fanned my enthusiasm and love for what I do, reciprocally making my work successful. What's more, I feel I that I can relate to anyone on any step of the corporate ladder because I have personally climbed the painstaking ascent from rung to rung, and sensed the unique feeling that comes along at each level.

SO, WHAT'S THE BOTTOM LINE?

The experiences that had the most influence on my career outlook was the one I had at the ground level. Following my education at the Fashion Institute of Technology (FIT), I started out as an intern for ArtScroll/Mesorah – an established publishing company. My job was to design book covers and book page layout, in the days before desktop publishing. Using a typesetting and stat machine, rubylith and an xacto blade, I assisted in the production of nearly 100 publications. The company was a large one, renowned for its high standards of accuracy and quality craftsmanship.

It was there that I gained an appreciation for typography and graphic design, and how its proper use can truly affect its readers. It was there that I learned how to juggle multiple tasks and deal with real-world pressures and production deadlines. I came to appreciate the wisdom of the written word and the inherent power it bestows on its masters, allowing them to communicate effectively with others. *Most importantly, I learned that it pays to be a perfectionist.* And that a bit of sweat and elbow grease never hurt anyone – hard work can be rewarding.

Looking ahead, I knew that I wanted to make my mark on others with a career as a marketing professional. In 1992 I created my own start-up company, *Bottom Line Marketing Group (then Bottom Line Design),* and built it up to the success that it is. It is there that I serve as the Chief Executive Officer to this day.

I have had the fortuity to share the wisdom that I have gained, with the people I have influenced throughout this juncture of my life's journey. I've bolstered the growth of innumerable brands, business and nonprofit organizations, holding their hands through their successes and challenges. I also feel fortunate to have been involved in collectively generating over $250,000,000 in revenue for my clients, over the past 25 years, and to have interacted with many notable personalities over that period.

By interacting and advising other business owners, I gained insight into the dynamics of business life and marketing. If asked to pinpoint the most essential lesson from the past two-and-a-half decades of my career that summarizes my philosophy of business, it would be: **In this day and age, countless companies are method-obsessed, and fail to focus on the true outcome they desire. To flourish amidst the muddle of the fast-paced business world, you have to be forward-focused. It's easy to trip and miscalculate your route, consuming copious amounts of time, resources and capital, merely due to a lack of purpose and destination. Yes, to grow your bottom line, you must work from the bottom up. But only as long as every step is guided by the bottom line – the shape of the overall outcome, rather than getting lost in the hustle of the steps that get you there.**

In short: planning is critical and strategy is crucial, but the bottom line is execution. And that is why I called my firm "Bottom Line Marketing Group."

I have observed firsthand the benefit of employing "Bottom Line" thinking, in terms of its ability to attain a nearly obsessive focus on execution, and producing a desired result.

Before I knew it, my start-up business met with success (and challenges), and I now found myself at the helm of an intensely dynamic marketing firm. We continue to think about our "Bottom Line" – that our goal is to see the company thriving at a level that would go beyond the zones of the niche of clientele we had become accustomed to servicing. We felt that we had provided for them in the best manner we could, and we were ready to spread our wings further. This mandated setting higher standards and implementing new action steps to meet the vision of breadth that reinvigorated our entire company. Together with my handpicked staff members, we focus on "The Bottom Line" – to see our company champion amongst those in the greater creative industry. We are fixated on the euphoria that came with getting closer to achieving our new future. Our efforts are well-spent, and all of our endeavors have continued to propel us towards our dream.

Throughout my interactions with people, I've enjoyed advising people navigate complexities. Often, I found myself musing over a thought or coming up with in interesting solution, and wondering how it could assist others. I would jot a memo about it to myself, hoping it would become of use one day for the greater good. Eventually, these ideas formed the basis for the marketing columns I authored in the Yated - a national weekly newspaper. My column was well-received, further allowing me to assist many through the extended reach of the medium. The tips became further popular, and my readership growth burgeoned with the inclusion of thousands of contacts via email. My ideas have also been put forward at the various conferences and venues that I've been invited to lecture at. And most recently, in the summer of 2015, I've been honored to host a business and marketing radio show on WABC, AM770 in New York City.

Over time, I have found that my advice for the "Bottom Line" approach for business owners can easily be achieved by closely adhering to certain basic ideas and strategies. These ideas formulate and represent the many facets of professional development and business life, and are the basis of the chapters of this book:

Chapter 1: Business Strategies for Success

Chapter 2: Effective Communication

Chapter 3: Out of the Box Marketing

Chapter 4: Execution

Chapter 5: Marketing Basics

Chapter 6: Marketing Initiatives

Chapter 7: Sustaining Your Business – Customer Retention

Chapter 8: Strategic Planning

It is this that I have compiled into a collection of articles, playfully dubbed, *"So, What's the Bottom Line?"* And so, the book you find in your hands was born. It is a personal work that essentially encapsulates the ideas, experiences, practices and beliefs that have empowered me over the past 25 years in the field of business and marketing.

These collected thoughts have not only been realized through personal encounters of discovery and experimentation of different approaches and methods; rather, they have stood the test of time. Additionally, they remain constant and correct in various business environments and circumstances, albeit, each with their own unique challenges. Above all, they were integral to my success.

I fervently hope that they will be advantageous to you, and help guide you in achieving your vision and life goals.

Yitzchok Saftlas
New York

ACKNOWLEDGEMENTS

Give thanks to G-d, for He is good, His kindness is forever. (Psalms 118)

People who interact with me on a daily basis know that I'm quite happy, and would be classified as an optimist. People have asked me, "What is the 'secret sauce' for maintaining your constant level of happiness and optimism?"

The secret to true happiness, is appreciation and gratitude. And, it is impossible to begin any conversation of appreciation, without thanking the one who created us all – G-d. When a person contemplates the gift of eyesight, the ability to walk, talk, hear, breathe deeply...and thinks about the endless list of gifts that G-d granted, how can an individual *not* be happy beyond words! I therefore take this opportunity to thank G-d for all the gifts in general, and now in particular, for granting me the ability to publish the book that you now hold in your hands.

Publishing a book requires the assistance of a great team. I first wish to thank my wife Esther and our precious children, my parents, Rabbi and Mrs. Chaim Saftlas and my in-laws, Mr. & Mrs. Gordon Weiser for their constant support and encouragement.

Next, I wish to thank the wonderful team at Bottom Line Marketing Group, whom I have the pleasure of working together with every day. They include: Bryna Bendel, Yitzi Bohensky, Yaakov Gerber, Chaya Litvintchouk, Pesach Tropper, Miriam Saftlas, Sruly Saftlas, Dini Schmulevitz and Aliza Ungar. Special thanks go to Yaakov Gerber, Pesach Tropper and Aliza Ungar; Aliza for the masterful cover design and icons that appear before each chapter; Yaakov for the entire layout; and to Pesach for naming this book and shepherding along the entire process.

A special thank you goes out to the people who have invested much time and effort into my development. They include: Rabbi Sheah Brander, Rabbi Yechezkel Eichenstein, Rabbi Dr. Zelig Friedman, Rabbi Avrohom Fruchthandler, Rabbi Eliezer Ginsburg, Rabbi Dovid Goldwasser, Rabbi Dovid Hofstedter, Rabbi Mordechai Kamenetzky, Rabbi Yitzchak Kasnett, Rabbi Paysach Krohn, Rabbi Avigdor Miller, Rabbi Yisroel Reisman, Rabbi Simcha Scheinberg, Rabbi Yeruchim Shain, Rabbi Nochum Stilerman, Rabbi Nosson Scherman, Rabbi Dovid Trenk, and Rabbi Meir Zlotowitz.

Next, I wish to thank a very special individual, whose idea was the foundation for this book: Rabbi Pinchos Lipschutz. He contacted me in 2009, with a creative yet straightforward idea, "Yitzchok," he said, "the economy is really rough and people can use some good marketing ideas, perhaps you want to pen a weekly business marketing column for the Yated Ne'eman?" And as the saying goes, "the rest is history!" This book is culled from the very best columns that appeared.

I deeply appreciate the close friends who reviewed the manuscript and were kind enough to pen some kind words about this book. They are: Jonathan Gassman, CPA/PFS CFP CAP, David J. Lieberman, Ph.D., Bill O'Reilly and noted business personality and congressman, the Honorable Robert L. Turner, who penned the forward that graces this book.

Additional thanks go out to friends who always have been extremely supportive of my work. They include: Eli Abbott, Menachem Adelman, R' Zev Bald, Sruli Besser, R' Tzvi Bider, R' Richard Chaim Bieler, R' Avrohom Birnbaum, R' Zvi Bloom, Shimmy Blum, Marc Bodner, Avi Bree, Chaim Brown, Hon. Noach Dear, Jeff Deutsch, R' Eli Dessler, Dennis Eisenberg, Jacob Engel, Mordy Ettinger, R' Moshe Ferber, Hon. Simcha Felder, Baila Feuerstein, George Flowers, Yehoshua Fox, Michael Fragin, Rechy Frankfurter, Rabbi Yitzchok Frankfurter, Yaakov and Rochel Esther Friedler, Howard Tzvi Friedman, Saul N. Friedman, Yaakov Shimon Friedman, Orly Gadayev, Shai Ghermezian,

R' Ahron Gobioff, Hon. Phillip Goldfeder, Sharon Green, Hon. David Greenfield, Hon. Dov Hikind, Aron Hirtz, Moshe Horowitz, R' Noson Joseph, R' Yitzi Kessock, Shalom Lamm, Avi Lazar, R' Nachman Levine, Mrs. Ruth Lichtenstein, Adam Lieberman, Aharon Melool, R' Naftali Miller, Yonason Moller, Aryeh Norensberg, Isaac Nutovic, Yossi and Susan Ostreicher, Jessica Proud, Avi Revah, Ben Rose, Shea Rubenstein, R' Baruch Rothman, Hon. Leon Ruchelsman, R' Eli Saftlas, Tzvi Saftlas, R' Uri Saftlas, Zev Saftlas, Ahron Schachter, David and Sharon Schild, Russell Schmidt, Dovid Schloss, R' Avi Shulman, Nachum Segal, Deidre Siegel, Marty Siegmeister, R' Wolf Sicherman, Yossi Sicherman, Dan Sullivan, Jose Torres, Aaron Troodler, Naftali Ungar, Tanya Voytovech, Isaac Wagschal, Miriam L. Wallach, Izzy Wasser, R' Meir Leib Yanofsky, and Ira Zlotowitz. Each person listed really deserves their own paragraph.

Finally, I wish to thank the great team at Morgan James Publishing: Jessica Foldberg, David Hancock, Jim Howard, Bethany Marshall, Nickcole Watkins, and W. Terry Whalin.

And finally, I thank you, the reader, for picking up this book and allowing me to share some business and marketing life lessons with you.

With appreciation,

Yitzchok Saftlas

BUSINESS STRATEGIES *for* SUCCESS

> If I had eight hours to chop down a tree,
> I'd spend six sharpening my axe.
>
> — Abraham Lincoln

THOU SHALT _be_ PREPARED

A true professional is always equipped with the tools of his trade to spring into action at a moment's notice. In addition to making a positive impression, preparation sets you apart from the competition and can help get your name in the public eye.

American Express has made a veritable fortune since the 1975 inception of its advertising campaign: "don't leave home without it." In addition to being a moneymaker and a memorable slogan that is now inseparable from American Express, it is also a solid piece of general advice.

A few years ago, I snapped a shot of a sign outside of a synagogue in Stamford Connecticut which says: "Thou Shalt Not Park Here." You may have seen it.

I took it one morning when I was in the area for a professional seminar. It may not be the 11th commandment, but I related to it with all earnestness, making sure not to park anywhere near that revered spot.

The key point here is that the only reason I was able to capture this shot on my digital camera, is simply because I had my camera with me. This is not rocket science. I always take a camera wherever I travel. Photography is an essential tool of the marketing trade, and

2

speaking of credits, the idea of never leaving home without my camera must be credited to Mr. Irving Schild.

Mr. Schild was one of my instructors when I attended FIT for advertising and marketing, many years ago. He is a world renowned photographer whose clients include a number of Fortune 500 companies. He is as nice of a man as you would ever want to meet. He taught us that if we wanted to be truly great photographers, we had to be camera-ready at all times. Nowadays, this is much easier. Most digital cameras and smart phones fit neatly into your shirt pocket and produce print quality photos.

I heard a similar story about being a "Johnny on the spot," involving Walter Rodgers, a former top CBS news correspondent. In March of 1981, just a couple of months after Ronald Reagan became president, a deranged man, John Hinckley Jr., tried to assassinate Reagan on the streets of Washington DC. Rodgers was the only radio reporter to get the sound of the gunshots on tape; giving CBS radio news a scoop.

How did he do it? He had left his tape recorder running the whole time he was out on the street to capture background noise. While most reporters would only turn on their tape at the start of an interview, Rodgers's standard practice was to press the record button every time he was out in public. After all, tape was cheap, you could always recharge the batteries once you got back to the office and you never knew what sounds you might pick up.

If it sounds simple — it's because it is! Sometimes the simplest preparations pay surprising dividends.

I would offer the same sound advice to anyone whose job responsibilities include meeting with the public and getting your name, or your organization's name across. I'm still surprised, on occasion, when I attend a conference or meeting and exchange business cards with the person I am meeting, only to hear him say he doesn't have one on him.

It is easy to be a bit complacent about business cards in this email / social media generation, but a good old-fashioned hearty handshake, smile, and handing out of a business card is still the best introduction.

Speaking of handouts, it can also pay off handsomely to have a tri-fold, color brochure of your organization handy to pull out of your jacket pocket that will fit just as perfectly inside the jacket pocket of the fellow you just shook hands with.

BOTTOM LINE ACTION STEP:
Have the tools of your trade handy at all times.

4

GREATLY APPRECIATED

Most of us were taught as children that please, and thank you, were magic words. They remain so for children, and all the more so when we reach adulthood.

The power of a simple thank you in the business world can send your stock soaring to new highs. Christopher Duffy, director of client and business development for Hogan – an international authority in personality assessment and consulting – once labeled himself "the unconsciously competent manager." He attributed that to the fact that he has incorporated thank you into his daily business vocabulary.

"I live for pats on the back," wrote Duffy. "They keep me motivated and are a much appreciated reward for a job well done." He also makes sure to reciprocate. "I do my best to ensure everyone on my team is recognized for a job well done. I do this through a variety of different mediums; verbally, publicly, in an email, a personal note, or through some type of gift."

While saying thanks can keep you in good graces with your clients, current employer and co-workers, it can also give you a boost when it comes to landing your "dream position," which is often no easy feat in the current economic climate. Joyce Russell, director of the Executive Coaching and Leadership Development Program at the University of Maryland's Robert H. Smith School of Business related the following story in the Washington Post's Career Coach column. A corporate recruiter received more than 3,000 applications for 200 available positions. Only one of those applicants bothered to send the recruiter a follow-up thank you note for her assistance in the job search process. Who do you think the recruiter thought of first when a suitable position opened up?

BOTTOM LINE ACTION STEP:

Just keep saying thank you...and watch the results!

THE TIMES
DEMAND URGENCY

At one time or another, many of us have probably said that we prefer not to work under pressure. Undue pressure, without a cause or a goal, is worth avoiding, but pressure born from urgency and ambition can be a positive and driving force of energy for your organization.

As I glance at the clock while finishing up an assignment, the sweat pouring down my brow has nothing to do with the hot weather.

It's the pressure of meeting yet another weekly deadline that keeps me sweating, knowing that an entire crew of editors, proofreaders and printers are waiting for me, and many others like me, to submit their work in a timely fashion. But just as exercise makes one sweat and doctors say this is healthy and beneficial to one's physical well-being, the perspiration that flows from the thought of having to meet – and beat – another deadline can also keep your business or non-profit organization in the best of fiscal shape.

Advertising and fundraising campaign deadlines and built-in pressures; it is the nature of the beast, so to speak. Whether it becomes a beast of burden or whether you harness it to your advantage is contingent upon how you approach it. What I have found over the years is that things only begin to start moving once you set a deadline. If an organization is planning a dinner, you must set a date first. The obvious reason is because you have to reserve a hall, a caterer, etc., and also because you want the attendees and the honorees to save the date. But the date also gives you a goal to work toward and we need goals to get us moving. Why does a business have a fiscal year?

To know when it has to close the books and make an accounting to shareholders and directors. Why do salespeople have monthly bonuses? So that when they near the end of the month, they will have an incentive to make that extra call, or call back to try and close a sale.

A few years ago, Harvard Professor John Kotter wrote a book: *A Sense of Urgency*, which reached #7 on the New York Times best seller list one month after it was published. Professor Kotter today has his own consulting firm. One of his titles is chief innovation officer. (Now that's a title I like!) Every organization can use someone like that.

His book focuses on what a true sense of urgency in an organization really is; why it is becoming an important asset and how it can be created and sustained. One of Professor Kotter's theories is that there are two types of change: episodic change that revolves around a single big issue such as a new product launch or acquisition and continuous change, which is a ceaseless flow of a combination of changes.

His premise is that the world itself has been transformed and has entered an era of continuous change. "With this shift," writes Professor Kotter, "urgency will move from being an important issue every few years to being a powerful asset all the time. The urgency question is not limited to any particular class of organization or group. Insufficient urgency... can undermine a plant, an office, or a whole country. Conversely, in all of these situations, a high sense of urgency can help produce results, and a whole way of life, that we all desire.

"It all begins with a high enough sense of urgency among a large enough group of people. Get that right and you are off to a great start. Get that right and you can produce results that you very much want, and the world very much needs."

BOTTOM LINE ACTION STEP:
Beat your deadlines, but don't let your deadlines beat you.

GEARED UP & READY TO GO

Expecting the unexpected sounds like an oxymoron, but there is more than one good reason to devote time and energy to planning for contingencies.

New Yorkers who toughed it during 2010's record blizzard, as well as 2011's Hurricane Irene, and 2013's Superstorm Sandy can immediately appreciate the difference being prepared makes.

When New York City was overwhelmed by two feet of snow, City Hall faced immense challenges mobilizing its crews to clear the streets. People were stuck inside for days while the crews cleared away the snow in a disorganized and slow fashion. In contrast, most observers gave the city top scores for their planned evacuation orders for Hurricane Irene. While some contend the Hurricane's evacuation orders were hasty and sparked by media hype, many scientists and civil engineers say the city's response made good sense. The evacuation plan was based on up-to-the-minute models of flood behavior, so the city's pro-activity might have saved thousands of lives had the worst case scenario occurred.

On my hurricane-delayed return to the office from upstate New York, I had some extra time to contemplate Irene and think about some of the lessons that could be gleaned from it. After considering how important it is for government agencies to prepare for every possible contingency, I realized how vital it can also be for businesses and even nonprofits to have contingency plans that allow them to leverage unexpected events related to their products, services, or areas of expertise.

Three days before Irene was projected to hit, while everyone was bracing for the coming storm, Home Depot ran a series of radio spots, positioning themselves as the one-stop outlet where consumers could stock up on materials that would keep their homes safe and sound.

I don't have any insider information here, but I would not be surprised if I discovered that Home Depot has ads such as these "in the can" that are ready to go in case disaster should strike regions where they have stores. And even if they just devised this ad campaign on the spot for Irene, it still demonstrates how important it is to have a team in place that can generate creative content at opportune times.

The GEICO insurance company is another prime example. The headline on their website said it all: *"GEICO Catastrophe Teams Are Ready to Help."*

Sure, they are an insurance company and they are in the business to write policies. But in addition to aiming for more business, their website was chock full of useful information on how to protect your life and property when severe weather threatens. They had links to hurricane preparedness sites and to the Center for Disease Control. They let people know that GEICO's Catastrophe Claims Response Teams had been deployed along the East Coast to assist policyholders affected by Hurricane Irene and that claims adjusters would remain in affected areas as long as necessary to take care of them.

There is another important lesson here. Home Depot or GEICO are certainly stirred by the profit motive, but they understand that the best way to reach people's wallets is by getting in touch with their hearts or their heads first. Showing concern for your customer is smart business in addition to good plain common decency.

No matter what business you may be in or what organization you represent, it is clearly beneficial to have contingency plans of your own on hand when events break in a way that you can benefit from. Of course, they have to be devised with common sense and tact to be extraordinarily careful to ensure that they don't have the slightest whiff of trying to take advantage of someone's misfortune.

Home Depot and GEICO did it by positioning themselves firmly on the customer's side and letting them know they were a reliable source of useful products and information.

In case you ask, what happens if I don't have a marketing budget at that moment to seize the opportunity, this is indeed a fair question.

Just as it is always wise to have some savings in the bank for a rainy day, it is also a good idea to keep some marketing or advertising revenues in reserve for a rainy day, that hopefully in the future will only bring success to your business.

BOTTOM LINE ACTION STEP:

Leap ahead in response to unfolding events,
rather than letting them throw you for a loss.

MARKETING ASIDE...
SOME GRATITUDE

Thank You!

Mucho Gracias!

Merci Beaucoup!

There are so many ways to express feelings of genuine thanks and appreciation. Transcending across nationalities and cultures, offering thanks to those who have given of themselves and their resources is one of the most basic forms of humanity. And yes, even a form of advertising as well.

According to an article in The Huffington Post (February 13, 2009), a conglomeration of special interest groups within the healthcare and pharmaceutical industry launched a 10 million dollar advertising campaign to thank and applaud lawmakers – Democrats and Republicans alike – for voting to expand children's health care funding.

"Tell your Senator, thanks for standing up for our kids," the ad said, "and that now's the time to guarantee quality, affordable health care for all Americans."

The positive-reinforcement ad campaign tactic is something that progressive groups also did for Republican Senators who crossed party lines in voting for the stimulus package. In this case, one function of the 'thank you' ad is clearly to build broader support for the more extensive health reform legislation in the future.

Another quintessential example of utilizing the 'thank you' technique can be illustrated with the legendary advertising campaign of financial giant Paine Webber (now operating under the auspices of UBS and known as UBS Wealth Management USA). The "Thank You Paine Webber" theme campaign highlighted clients expressing their thanks and gratitude to Paine Webber for boosting their stock portfolios and improving their lives.

By having clients thanking Paine Webber in a genuine direct way, the ads were able to successfully convey the personal and caring approach utilized by the company to assist its clients. After all, what can be more authentic than a true, heartfelt 'thank you'?

BOTTOM LINE ACTION STEP:

Call up a big client and thank them for their business, they will probably thank you back.

 **"QPR"**

I was listening to a local Jewish radio show one morning and the host, Nachum Segal, was interviewing two renowned wine experts: Mr. Motty Herzog and Mr. Jay Buchsbaum of Kedem / Royal Wine Corporation.

While discussing the benefits of cabernet sauvignon, merlot and chardonnay proved to be enlightening, I personally found the discussion about Kedem's "Quality-Price Ratio" or "QPR" to be most fascinating.

"QPR" is a marketing term that describes the overall value of a product in comparison to its price. During the radio show, Mr. Herzog emphasized how Kedem's Baron Herzog is a value line that has been rated as a top-quality wine which is easily affordable. He pointed out that although there are comparable products in a lower price category, when you factor in the value of the Baron Herzog product, it's a fantastic value. Hence, the "QPR" makes it a fantastic buy.

14

You needn't be in the wine business to appreciate the uniqueness of having a "QPR" as part of your marketing mix. It plays a critical role in deciding how to portray, price and market a product – and how consumers will react to the product itself.

On his blog, marketing consultant Chuck McKay expertly explains the differentiations caused by having a defined "QPR." For example, Walmart is positioned as the lowest price retailer. Therefore, products in Walmart are priced as cheaply as possible and are generally not portrayed as luxurious or upscale. Target, on the other hand, has a more sophisticated image of a fashionable discounter – and it shows. Target's ads, promotions, products and even store designs have a certain fashionable and hip feel to them.

Therefore, being that Target exudes a more refined image, consumers are willing to pay a bit more for a metal picture frame that may have actually been manufactured in the same plant as Walmart's picture frames. However, because Target boasts a higher "QPR," they can charge a bit more than Walmart would for picture frames – and the consumer will gladly pay it.

BOTTOM LINE ACTION STEP:

Whether your company features a product or service,
be sure to position and market it properly to command
the appropriate price model and fee structure.

We all know the famous saying, "Humans were created with two ears and one mouth." It therefore makes sense that we should spend twice as much time listening than talking! While it takes training and self-discipline to achieve the correct ratio, many have perfected the art. Sales and marketing people can definitely learn from them.

In this day and age, many professional marketing techniques have become universally accepted in the world and have been employed to raise significant sums for organizations. Marketing is an academic discipline, a profession and a business. However, when applied to non-profit organizations, then such work becomes lofty as well.

Recently, I came across an article that reinforced my appreciation for how warmth and empathy can coexist seamlessly with success in business.

Clay Forsberg, a corporate recruiter and sales coach, penned a piece in Printing Impressions, a trade publication for commercial printers. (A quick thank you goes out to Mrs. Gitty Ostreicher of Edison Litho, who brought this article to my attention). Mr. Forsberg's style is forthright; his opening premise of "don't fool yourselves, your customers don't care about you" is a challenge to all business people to sit up straight in their chairs and think.

For those of us who are used to pleasantries, camaraderie and even going to ball games with our clients, such a line comes off as a bit of a shock. What does he mean "my customers don't care about me?" Didn't they just invite me to a holiday party? Doesn't that prove that he cares about me?

While it's true that salespeople and customers may attend each others' parties or perhaps tee off together, Forsberg is coming to remind us that *what our customers really care about is what our product or service will do for them and their lives.* "The best way to learn this is to listen. By listening, rather than pitching, you'll find out what's important to them, and what they'll react to." This may seem elementary, but it really cuts right to the core of the issue. When Forsberg says your average customer doesn't care about you, he is explaining that customers can be very cold-blooded and calculating. A salesperson must demonstrate that their own service or product will deliver for them, that you really understand them and care about *them.*

"Imagine if one of your suppliers took the time to get to know you – really get to know you. Would you do business with them? *Would you let that person into your life?* I'm betting you would," says Forsberg.

BOTTOM LINE ACTION STEP:
Be a great listener and observe the impact on your professional growth.

CAN WE REALLY DO 17 THINGS *at* ONCE?

Attention spans aren't what they used to be, which presents a modern-day dilemma that creates new challenges for all of us. This presents a greater challenge for companies and organizations which thrive by ensuring that their messages are seen and heard. How can we grab people's attention when they are bombarded from all directions?

You never get a second chance to make a first impression.

We have all heard that expression before. But in this era of information overload, you only have a critical three seconds to make that first impression. That's all it takes anymore for the consumer or reader to decide if he is interested in hearing more. That impression might be made by the sound or tone of your voice, the headline on an advertisement, or even the choice of colors and pictures. Three seconds is all you have to get your target audience to focus on you and have your message click with them.

Many people bemoan this state of affairs and pine for a simpler era, when we slept on feather pillows, and not with an iphone, android or BlackBerry on the night table, but you just can't turn the clock back.

I got a greater appreciation of both the problem, and a potential solution, while perusing an article in McKinsey Quarterly that both caught, and held my attention, for 3000 words – much longer than three seconds. McKinsey and Co. are realists. They didn't glorify multi-tasking or take multi-taskers to task. They did give solid pointers on how some top 21st century executives are managing to cope with a flood of information and not drown in it.

Perhaps most insightfully, McKinsey gave us a glimpse of what it takes to get the attention of busy people.

The root of the problem, according to McKinsey, is that when we switch between tasks, especially complex ones, we become startlingly less efficient. A recent study showed that participants who completed tasks in parallel fashion took up to 30 percent longer and made twice as many errors as those who completed the same tasks in sequence. The delay comes from the fact that our brains can't successfully tell us to perform two actions concurrently.

Unlike red wine, multi-tasking does not improve with age and we don't get better with experience. Heavy multi-taskers take even longer to switch between tasks than occasional multi-taskers.

Since it always seems as if we are multi-tasking in this day and age, it is now clearer why we sometimes have trouble concentrating on or relating to another piece of information that comes our way. There is hope, however, but not unless your piece of info really hits the bulls-eye.

Gary Loveman, CEO and president of Harrah's Entertainment told McKinsey that you can gain his time, but "you need to do some work" [in advance] and "provide me with data and insight…"

Christine Beasley, England's Chief Nursing Officer took a similar view: "You cannot read everything. The things that I do look at are the things that matter, the things I really need to make a decision on."

McKinsey also noted that in their conversations with Loveman, Beasley and other CEOs, executing strategies in our "always-on" environment requires a tremendous amount of self-discipline, and can't be done alone.

Collaboration really works. Teresa Amabile and her colleagues at the Harvard Business School analyzed 9,000 workers in creative fields and found that the likelihood of creative thinking is higher when people focus on one activity for a significant part of the day and collaborate with just one other person.

The same notions can be applied to marketing and advertising. Just as you need a doctor to diagnose you and an accountant to give you tax advice, you can't market or publicize alone. In an era where attention spans are taxed as much as our wallets, marketing is a collaborative effort; best done in consultation with a marketing firm that will craft a message that is creative, insightful, informative and gets it across in a way that matters to busy decision-makers.

BOTTOM LINE ACTION STEP:
Take out time to focus.
Then develop your message to resonate above the clutter!

EDUCATING *your* DONOR BASE

While many non-profits face the challenge of covering severe budget gaps, New York's Fordham University broke its own fundraising record – astonishingly, during the recent severe recession. Raising a record-breaking 67.4 million dollars in new pledges and gifts – an increase of 39% over the previous year! Fordham University has shown that with the right ideas, planning and people, successful fundraising campaigns are always possible.

According to an article in the premier business magazine, Crains New York, the university was in the middle of a $500 million fundraising campaign to build new facilities, offer scholarships to more students and expand academic offerings. The campaign was spearheaded by volunteers, most of whom are members of the Board of Trustees. In a press release highlighting the details of this campaign, Trustee James E. Buckman, Esq. explained the underlying mechanisms behind the successful results.

"Volunteers are critical to the campaign," Buckman said. "Their role is threefold: to demonstrate leadership with their own financial commitment to the campaign; to actively lead the solicitation efforts by identifying people who can provide substantive support to the University, and aid in soliciting donations from them; and in helping other core volunteers in the overall fundraising effort."

Mr. Buckman also noted that alumni who are themselves significant contributors have an edge in recruiting donors. "Having given themselves, they are confident in expressing their commitment to the campaign."

Most importantly though, Al Checcio, Fordham's vice president for development and university relations, clearly articulated the primary reason why the campaign has been so successful. "Even in one of the toughest economic climates I've seen in my career, our trustee volunteers and professional staff have been able to convey the importance of Fordham's mission and the need to support that mission financially," he said.

That statement is really quite revealing. Let's review it again: "Even in one of the toughest economic climates I've seen in my career, our trustee volunteers and professional staff *have been able to convey the importance of Fordham's mission and the need to support that mission financially.*"

In essence, Mr. Chiccio is saying what every seasoned fundraiser knows all too well: toot your own horn. Educate your donor base, staff, alumni, parent body, board members, etc., about your day-to-day work, your mission and message, and they will respond.

In addition, they will be familiar enough with your message to "toot your horn" and educate others about *your* message. Whether it's a board member making a solicitation from his business partner, an honoree from his friends and neighbors, etc., having a band of loyal horn-tooters is a surefire way to continuously get an organization's message across and ultimately generate funds.

But first things first – you have to give them what to toot about.

Launching a new program? Hired a new star on your staff? Reaching an impressive milestone? Let supporters know what's going on and emphasize the significance of it. How do you accomplish that? Newsletters, press release, advertisements, CD audio/visual presentations...the methods are endless! And of course, remember to stay true to your organization's mission and identity in all outgoing marketing materials.

A few general tips that will positively affect your fundraising efforts:

- Marketing a non-profit organization is all about reaching numerous people with a compelling message – a powerful message that will inspire them to take immediate action and assist your organization.

- Make your organization's mission and message more powerful by giving it a story-like, visual image that speaks to people's emotions.

- Most importantly (as gleaned from Fordham University's successful campaign), keep volunteers fresh and motivated! Establish a thought-out fundraising plan that maximizes the value of people's resources, time and energy.

Because after all, whether one has a PhD, Masters Degree or just a high school diploma, Fordham University has proven that there's still much for us to learn about the never-ending lessons of successful fundraising!

BOTTOM LINE ACTION STEP:

When times are tough and the economy is down, use volunteers and every business associate to toot your business' or organization's horn.

23

WONDERS & MIRACLES

One of the most important elements of marketing is continuously reminding the public about your product or service by publicizing it. Your business performs wonders and miracles for your clients day-in-and-day-out. Doesn't it? Your non-profit organization performs wonders and miracles day and night. If you don't publicize it through marketing, no one will ever appreciate it. Out-of-sight, out-of-mind! If you don't publicize it, then your current and prospective clients will never appreciate it!

A prominent economist named Roland Vaile apparently understood this concept quite well. He conducted a study that proved the following point: the more a business spends on marketing itself, the more profits it will generate. Mr. Vaile found that in the recession of 1921-22, companies that kept their ad spending stable or increased it saw their sales hold up significantly better than those that didn't.

In more recent years, a Korean car company called Hyundai made huge gains in market share by upping their advertising budget and publicizing a guarantee to take back cars from owners who lost their jobs. According to Advertising Age, after launching an intensive 115 million dollar marketing campaign at the beginning of 2009, Hyundai's sales jumped by 27% – while General Motors, Ford and Chrysler

24

simultaneously posted record sales losses of 22%. Talk about the benefits of publicizing a product!

A common refrain I often hear – especially when businesses attempt to weather an economic downturn – is that advertising during an economic downturn is pointless. "Nobody is spending money now," people scoff. "Why bother advertising in a down economy?" Well, history shows otherwise.

According to an article in The New Yorker, the uncertainty of economic downturns creates tremendous marketing opportunities for those seeking to generate serious profits. The historical record is full of companies that took advantage of advertising during recessions. The Kraft Food Company launched a new line of salad dressing during the Great Depression known as Miracle Whip. With a highly publicized ad campaign in place, Miracle Whip became America's bestselling dressing in just six months.

Steve Jobs of Apple rolled out a little white device known as an iPod with great fanfare during the 2001 dot-com bubble collapse. With a memorable advertising campaign that boasted the ability of "Putting 1,000 songs in your pocket", it has been hailed as one of the most successful product launches ever.

And of course, there is the legendary tale of how Kellogg's gained a 30% market share over its competitor, Post Cereal, during the Great Depression by doubling its ad budget – all while the competition slashed their marketing budget.

Bottom line? The only proven way to grow a company and generate profits is by continuously reminding consumers of your product or service by publicizing it. How do you go about doing that? Well, as the previous cases clearly illustrate, by ensuring your entity has a serious advertising and marketing plan in place.

Oh, and about that 115 million dollar campaign launched by Hyundai? Don't let the numbers frighten you. Today's marketing agencies specialize in developing customized campaigns tailored for companies of all sizes and budgets. So take out that pad, grab a pen, and start jotting down all the ways your business performs wonders and miracles for its clients. Then, contact a professional marketing firm and publicize it; and yes, the clients will follow!

BOTTOM LINE ACTION STEP:
Step up your marketing efforts, even when the economy is down.

BUILDING WORLDS
with WORDS

Life presents us with many growth opportunities, including building our homes, our careers, our families and ourselves. Organizations are also dynamic, just like people. By showing their supporters and the public how they are growing, they perform an important service to the community and to donors.

It would be wonderful if every parent could periodically visit their children's schools to view the dedication of the teachers and the administration in real time.

For most of us, this is impossible, due to our own personal and professional commitments. The administrators are aware of this and that is one reason they invest the time, effort and even the funds to raise community awareness of their ongoing accomplishments and challenges.

Recently, the creative team at Bottom Line Marketing Group was privileged to work alongside an educational institution on a commemorative book to coincide with the opening ceremony for their glorious, new $31-million building. This undertaking resulted in the production of a 192-page stunning, coffee-table sized volume, "Building Worlds," which was distributed to some 2000 attendees. The book contained six chapters of the school's history, a fascinating written piece, elaborating on the history and mission of the school, captivating photos and a section recognizing the commitment of the school's many generous donors.

Obviously, the investment that went into this book was an expense that had to be carefully weighed to ensure that its ultimate value would be greater than the cost. This is the obvious dilemma that every organization must grapple with, and even justify, before spending precious funds. (Although I must add that in almost all cases, a generous donor sponsors the marketing costs – as happened in this case).

In our era, distribution of informational material is the only way by which an organization can get its message out of the office and into a donor's home. It is their way of giving honor to the mission; by keeping you informed of their accomplishments, goals and needs and to show you the ways in which you can contribute to their cause, if you choose to do so.

There is another value-added concept at play here. By creating and distributing institutional material, an organization forces itself to appraise its strengths, gaining a greater appreciation for all of its efforts and hard work.

In the process, the organization provides encouragement to itself, and to vital organization insiders, including the board of directors, the volunteers and the dedicated staff. This positive reinforcement boosts morale and reverberates throughout the organization.

BOTTOM LINE ACTION STEP:

Give rein to your organization to promote itself appropriately and take pride in its day-to-day and long-term accomplishments. Raise awareness in the community of what you have done and what you need to do next.

EFFECTIVE COMMUNICATION

> *You can have brilliant ideas, but if you can't get them across, your ideas won't get you anywhere.*
>
> - Lee Iococca

SECRETS *of* GREAT LEADERS

How do the finest leaders motivate and inspire their followers? How do the leading non-profits position themselves as worthy causes? And, how do profitable companies promote their products and services in today's highly competitive markets?

Hearing my computer ping with the familiar sound of an incoming e-mail, I eagerly click on my inbox to see who is writing me. Maybe it's an important client with a key piece of information? Perhaps it's a potential new client inquiring about my services?

Sometimes, to my great disappointment, it is a piece of correspondence that bounced back due to an incorrect or incomplete e-mail address. If it's my mistake, I can easily check it out and correct it. But what happens if the intended recipient erred and gave me a wrong address? Depending on where I met the person, it can be difficult to find his correct contact information.

America's top executives are expected to master all of the six basic functions of management: leading, planning, organizing, staffing, controlling and communicating, says Lee Froschheiser, president and CEO of Map Consulting and coauthor of the best seller: *"Vital Factors, The Secret to Transforming Your Business – And Your Life."*

While all six are vital, Froschheiser says clear communication is the golden thread that ties all of these functions together: "Think about it ... how do the best leaders motivate and inspire their people? Through clear communication. How do the best organizations promote discipline, accountability and strategic alignment? With clear communication. And, how do market leaders sell their products and services? With compelling ads and marketing campaigns — in sum, by clear communication."

Froschheiser shares some practical tips:

Clarify the goal of the communication at the outset, plan it carefully before sending it and anticipate the receiver's viewpoint and feelings.

Deliver the message with conviction, relate it to your larger goals, identify the action to be taken and confirm that the other person understands.

Be receptive. Communication is a two-way street, so keep an open mind. Value constructive feedback and use it to grow and then confirm your understanding of the other person's correspondence. Froschheiser addressed the highlights; now I would like to tie up some loose ends. Some may seem very basic, but even professionals such as musicians and athletes must always drill on the basics to stay in shape.

If you are leaving a voice mail, speak clearly and be certain to leave complete contact information. Leave your full name, phone number and the approximate time that you called. Let the person know whether you would like him to return your call or whether you will call again. If you leave your contact information on a cell phone, repeat yourself if you can, in case background noise or garbled speech rendered some of your words incomprehensible.

Don't be hasty in shooting off an e-mail. Be your own editor. Read it over once or twice and place yourself in the recipient's seat. Will they understand what you mean? A lot of time can be wasted on back-and-forth e-mails to clarify intentions and sometimes to smooth out misunderstandings.

Finally, use abbreviations sparingly, if at all. Not everyone knows that BTW is by the way and not the newest NYC subway line.

BOTTOM LINE ACTION STEP:
Always communicate clearly.

MISSION IMPOSSIBLE?

One of the most important lessons in marketing was taught neither by an advertising professional nor a business professor. Rather, it was publicized by a sailor-turned-statesman during a cold-war era speech that has since been emblazoned into the pages of history books throughout the globe.

> *"We choose to go to the moon. We choose to go to the moon in this decade and do the other things, not because they are easy, but because they are hard..."*
>
> — President John F. Kennedy - September 12, 1962

This historical quote – intended to generate enthusiasm against the ideological battle with the Soviet Union – is priceless. It serves as more than just a political sound-bite; deeper than a philosophical statement; and infinitely more valuable than a mere political opinion. This powerful quote is a genuine exemplification of results-oriented planning and direction.

If nothing more, President Kennedy's precise vision enabled the USA to overcome the Russians in their quest to win the "Space Race." By setting a defined goal, the American Nation had a blueprint charted out for them; all they needed to do was follow it. Astronaut Neil Armstrong's stroll on the moon in 1969 was merely a culmination of the president's vision.

33

Now imagine for a moment that President Kennedy would have walked up to the podium, looked directly at the news cameras and said something to this effect:

"We plan on making space capsules that will boast many detailed electrical components. They will utilize advanced rocket thrusters to propel them through space. The space capsules will be equipped with heat shields that will protect them while reentering the atmosphere. Oh yeah, and we're gonna use them to send a few people to the moon."

Do you honestly think such a muddled, vague speech – chock full of facts, but devoid of substance or direction – would have given the rocket engineers at NASA proper guidance, inspiration and encouragement? Of course not! It is highly doubtful such a speech would have made it to the headlines of reputable newspapers, let alone to serve as the impetus of putting a man on the moon.

If there was one cardinal rule to be etched into the cornerstone of every institution or organization, it would be the lesson taught by President Kennedy: Market your mission, not your services!

Because strictly speaking, services may change and evolve with the times – but an entity's mission will almost always remain the same.

For example, a hospital's mission is to save people's lives. A hundred years ago, somebody with severe cardiac issues might have only received an unperfected, rudimentary surgical procedure to help alleviate the condition. In 2015, a person suffering from a serious cardiac condition, can opt for a stent, bypass surgery or even a heart transplant that will allow them to enjoy long and healthy lives. You see, the hospital's methods may have changed – but their mission of saving lives hasn't.

In the same vein, when an organization in its newsletter, advertisements and brochures, tries to woo potential donors with oodles of technical information such as: "We maintain a caring staff of over 35 special-education teachers", they are failing to captivate readers with an important message; rather it bores people with random facts that don't give over a specific point – and most importantly, doesn't urge recipients to donate.

Now if you were to take that exact same statement and transform it into a message that gives off a powerful vibe such as: "Our educators help disabled children learn to read and gain self confidence and independence", it clearly delineates what your organization's mission is and why it's important for the reader to take part in your important cause.

When renowned marketing guru, Alan Rosenspan, was hired by a large auto body repair shop to launch a marketing campaign in an industry thick with competition, he refrained from using the clichéd marketing language that others in the industry were using (such as: "Lots of experience!" or "Professional staff!"). Instead, he sent prospective customers a crumpled-up postcard with the following to-the-point sentence: "If your car looks like this, you should come to O'Neil's Body Shop!"

As you can see, this no-beating-around-the-bush headline zoomed in on what the company's mission was (e.g. to fix bashed up cars) and kept away from the side details which were obviously important to attract clients, but not the primary selling message (e.g. how many years in business, competency of staff, etc.).

It is of paramount importance for businesses and non-profits to focus on highlighting and emphasizing their mission on all marketing materials.

Because by having a defined mission that clearly conveys to people – be it clients with car wrecks or donors with wallets – what you do and why it concerns them, you transform others from being impossibly interested into possible profit-boosters.

BOTTOM LINE ACTION STEP:
Always communicate your mission, not just your services, to your customers, your clients or your donors.

35

TO TELL *the* TRUTH

What goes into conceiving a memorable campaign; one that makes your product or service into a household name, for years to come? We know that you have to be creative, but "creative" is a very broad term. Why is it that some advertising slogans stick with us long after the advertiser has moved on to his next campaign?

The answer is that the advertiser has succeeded in defining his product or service so that it touches the people they are trying to reach. Everyone wants to have a long life, correct? That's why you remember: "Coke Adds Life."

True, everyone's heard of Coca-Cola anyway, but what about Buckley's Cough Syrup? Unlike Coke, which tastes great, Buckley's slogan is: "It tastes awful... And it works."

Buckley's started making cough syrup in 1920 in Canada. In 2002, they sold their company for an undisclosed fortune to Novartis, one of the world's leading pharmaceutical firms. How did Buckley's succeed with something that tastes so foul? They told the truth about themselves. They admitted they taste awful, but when you have a hacking cough that's keeping you awake at night and disturbing all the neighbors too, you'll try almost anything...as long as it works.

Isabelle Albanese, a leading marketing consultant for Fortune 500 companies, and author of "The 4Cs of Truth in Communication," says that moving people is not magic - it's all about effective communication. Her 4C model stands for "Comprehension", "Connection", "Credibility", and "Contagiousness".

> *Comprehension* means to hone your message to a main point in order to make sure that it instantly communicates your point. Most importantly, this method effectively ensures that the audience can "play the message back." If they can, you can be sure that they "got it."

> *Connection* with a communicated idea or message means not only that the audience "gets it," but that it resonates with them, has meaning and significance, and triggers a response to spark new behaviors and actions.

> *Credibility* is where the truth comes into play. Your audience needs to believe *who* is saying it, *what* is being said, and *how* it is being said. Otherwise, any connection begins to break down - immediately. Credibility is the critical "C", says Isabelle.

> *Contagiousness:* To be contagious, says Isabelle, a message has to be energetic, new, different, and memorable. It should also evoke a vivid emotional response, have "talk" potential, motivate the target to do something, and elicit a demonstrable reaction.

BOTTOM LINE ACTION STEP:

Think about what really holds true for your product and service. Develop and hone your message around that truth.

CURING TOYOTA'S WOES WITH TYLENOL?

Toyota, the world's largest automaker, took a major step toward putting their woes behind them when the company agreed to a $1.2 billion settlement with the Justice Department over cases of unintended acceleration in millions of Toyota and Lexus vehicles.

The troubles began in 2009, when a family of five from San Diego were killed in an auto accident after their gas pedal jammed and they couldn't stop their car.

Business looked bleak for Toyota after the accident. The company's reputation for quality and reliability was severely tarnished. Coupled with the global recession, Toyota announced its first annual loss in 60 years.

Toyota still had issues. Shortly after the settlement, the company announced an additional recall of more than 6-million vehicles for a variety of defects. Toyota will have to correct those defects, and figure out what's going wrong in their quality control processes so they don't recur.

At the same time, Toyota's woes hammered home the role of a corporate communications department in issuing clear, factual and ongoing reports to the consumer public.

The general rule of thumb for good public relations practices in the wake of a disaster, says Kim Norton, a director at Fresh Start Communications, is to be sympathetic when accidents happen; take responsibility for company errors; be transparent and get the word out before others can twist it.

Toyota initially mishandled the communication in the wake of the fatal crash. It only issued a belated condolence message, it blamed a supplier for a faulty part that contributed to the accident, it initially denied that their cars had any defects, and they weren't proactive in providing information to the media that might have resulted in more balanced coverage.

Toyota then remodeled its image with its "Let's Go Places Safely" campaign. Internally, Toyota executives realized the importance of reassuring their workers that the company was still solid by holding regular meetings with its workforce and even sending text messages to employees to ensure they would be the first to know important goings-on inside the company.

By 2012, the company regained its position as the world's number one automaker, and held onto that slot in 2013.

While Toyota obviously learned from their own experiences, had they followed the model approach set by Johnson and Johnson almost 30-years earlier, they probably could have spared themselves a lot of damaging publicity.

In 1982, seven people in the Chicago region died after taking Tylenol pain-relief capsules that had been intentionally laced with potassium cyanide by an unknown killer.

Upon hearing the news, Tylenol immediately distributed warnings to hospitals, distributors and stores, and simultaneously halted Tylenol production. They issued a nationwide recall of all Tylenol products and advertised in the national media – at an expense of over 50 million dollars – alerting consumers not to consume any Tylenol products until the situation was resolved.

The executives at Tylenol clearly understood how to communicate with the public in times of disaster and were applauded in the media for being honest and transparent with the public.

Most importantly, realizing that the deaths occurred as a result of an unknown killer tampering with bottles on store shelves, Tylenol took a proactive approach to regain the trust of consumers by designing a revolutionary triple-sealed package that would prevent product tampering from occurring.

Coupled with an aggressive product re-launch, heavy price promotions and the positive image of having been honest with the public in a time of disaster, Tylenol's market share jumped from a dismal 8% to 35% in the year following the incident.

The Tylenol fiasco is now considered to be a textbook response for creating effective public relations solutions and is studied by business executives and marketers alike. In a nutshell, these are the three key attributes in Tylenol's successful handling of the situation:

Communication: By keeping the public informed of the problem and taking responsibility to ensure that nobody else would be affected by it, Tylenol created an image for itself as a company that genuinely cared about its customers – even at the expense of losing money. Tylenol communicated with the public via multiple venues including newspaper ads, radio commercials and press releases.

Transparency: Throughout the ordeal, Tylenol was in contact with the FBI and police authorities, giving over its resources and databases to help figure out how the problem originated. Tylenol also held daily news conferences updating the media on the latest occurrences, successfully keeping the public in the loop and building brand credibility in the process.

Responsibility: Tylenol immediately pulled all of its products off store shelves and instructed consumers to discard all Tylenol products. They also offered a $100,000 reward for the capture of the person responsible for lacing the Tylenol bottles with poison. Lastly, they made it their business to ensure that such a situation would never again occur by designing new bottles with a tamper-proof seal, reassuring consumers that all Tylenol products were 100% safe.

Lesson learned; every company should be prepared so that when necessary, they can handle even the most difficult of circumstances.

BOTTOM LINE ACTION STEP:
When doing "damage control," truthful consistent communication coupled with a proactive plan is the best public relations marketing strategy.

THE 11 "POWER WORDS" of MARKETING

Want to touch a piece of living history? Would you like to wrap your fingers around a historical object that will link the past with the present?

Okay, hold on to this book real tight. Don't let go. Do you feel the pages between your fingers? Good! You have just connected with an item that has been in existence for thousands of years – paper!

That's right, unlike computers, telephones and iPods, iPads, etc., paper is not a recent invention. Originally invented by the ancient Egyptians through converting fibers of the papyrus plant into flat sheets of writing material (hence the name *"paper"*), paper has been used over the centuries for correspondence, documentation and – what else? Advertising!

And just like the paper making process has undergone tremendous technological advances over the decades (when was the last time you saw a spiral notebook made of papyrus or mulberry leaf?), so has the advertising process. While olden-day advertisers needed no more than paper and ink to ply their trade, today's advertising and marketing professionals require a keen knowledge of fonts, linguistics and even human psychology.

Agencies today spend hours poring over every word that will be written in an ad or brochure. Every letter, nuance and adjective is thought out and discussed before it makes its way to the printing press. Indeed, the words utilized within modern-day corporate communications are extremely powerful and can spell the difference between a profitable sale – or a lost one.

A article that appeared in The Wall Street Journal titled, *"How to Sell a $35,000 Watch in a Recession,"* highlighted the important process that words play in the business and sales process.

Staff reporter, Ms. Christina Binkley, spent a day observing the salespeople of an upscale watch store in Beverly Hills, California. One of the most important observations gleaned from the WSJ article (from a marketing perspective) were their use of words – or substitution of words. For example, salespeople are told to never mention the word "price," as it can potentially turn off a customer ("The _price_ of this Rolex is $20,000."). They are rather urged to use the word "value" instead ("The _value_ of this Rolex is $20,000."). It may seem to be a small and subtle difference, yet that one word can spell the difference between success and failure.

Try this one. Remember how I referred to the aforementioned store as a watch store? Well, that was a big no-no. Upscale watch retailers don't sell watches; they sell timepieces. Remember, the product can be the same – it's the wording that makes it different.

When focusing on advertising to the masses, keep in mind the following word study done by Yale University. Researchers at the psychology department did a study to see how consumers reacted to certain words used in advertising.

The following 11 words (known as *power words*) scored the highest with regard to piquing consumer interest and transforming indifferent shoppers into enthusiastic clients. Here goes:

- *New* (this word is a marketing favorite – after all, everybody wants to see or have something that's a novelty!)

- *Save* (hey, who doesn't want to save time or money – especially in a recession.)

- *Safety* (this word's important – because consumers don't want to spend their mornings worrying if the toaster is going to zap them again!)

- *Proven* (where applicable of course, consumers don't want to be the 'guinea pig' of your product or service.)

- *Love* (we all love chocolate and ice cream!)

- *Discover* (this word offers clients a sense of excitement, adventure and anticipation!)

- *Guarantee* (provides buyers with a safety net that reassures them about the quality of the product they're about to purchase.)

- *Health* (everybody is concerned about their health – if the product can do something for it, let them know!)

- *Results* (help consumers rationalize their purchase – they'll feel better about opening their wallets if they know they're receiving results!)

- *You* (this word is an undisputed winner and listed as the most powerful word in every marketing study ever performed – talk directly to the consumer and get personal to make the sale! However, be careful not to misuse this word and speak to consumers in a commanding or domineering way which can potentially make them back off!)

Oh, the 11th word! There is one word that was not mentioned in this particular study but is nonetheless viewed as a magic bullet by marketers across the globe – the word *"Free!"* There you have it: the 11 power words of marketing that every company should be using in their corporate advertising and marketing efforts.

So please dear reader, feel **free** to **discover** the **proven** words that will **guarantee** amazing **results**, attract **new** clients and **save you** money (not bad, 8 words out of 11!).

Because as marketers know all to well, words are tremendously powerful and – when utilized properly – will generate revenue, boost profits and improve your company's fiscal **health**.

BOTTOM LINE ACTION STEP:

Choose words wisely – the right words can make all the difference in the world.

PUSH *the* ENVELOPE

Though only an inch wide by an inch high, there's nothing small about postage stamps.

They have indisputably opened the channels of communication for families, businesses and organizations worldwide. After all, who hasn't received a cherished birthday or anniversary card from a close relative; an important letter from a valuable client overseas; or a mailing from a local charity updating supporters on the important work they do?

Thanks to the advantages offered by direct-mail, thousands of organizations have been able to keep donors informed and generate contributions year after year. While in this essay I will be focusing on how non-profits can utilize this form of marketing to their advantage, keep in mind that direct-mailings can (and should!) be used by organizations, businesses and political campaigns alike.

Among the important decisions when launching a direct-mail campaign is the mailing's outer envelope. Will you be writing a catchy message on the front to grab the recipient's attention? How about a colorful or oversized envelope to ensure that your mailing will be seen and opened? There are many ways to make a mailing stand out amongst the pile of bills, letters and postcards haphazardly stuffed into your mailbox.

Often, organizations will have a brief headline on the envelope about their important work or the people they help, hoping to intrigue the reader's curiosity. However, be very careful what you write. According to Katherine Barr, a noted instructor for the Direct Marketers Association, one should never ask a question that someone can give a "yes" or "no" answer to.

For example, an organization should not write on an envelope: *"Do you want to help a poor child?"* Rather, they should write: *"Your gift today will help poor children tomorrow."*

The second example is much more powerful since it cannot easily be answered with a "no." Furthermore, it avoids having to ask a direct question to the reader by providing them with the answer. They are now in a frame of mind where the issue is not "yes" or "no" (where they are offered the ability to reject the mailing), but rather encourage them to "help now" (which hopefully encourages them to open the envelope).

Not long ago, Bottom Line Marketing Group used the size and color of a direct-mailing envelope to launch a successful direct-mail campaign for a client. Looking extremely similar to an oversized United States Postal Service priority envelope, recipients assumed the important-looking envelope sitting in their mailbox was – well, important.

They opened the document inside and read the contents carefully. How do we know? Based on positive response and feedback that the client received, it was obvious that our envelope design was the key element that captured the attention and interest of recipients.

But it wasn't *that* simple. The United States Postal Service has rules regarding the size, coloring and look of direct-mail envelopes. It takes years of experience and familiarity to design an effective outer envelope. (Always seek creativity by 'pushing the envelope,' excuse the pun).

Lastly, the crowning touch to any direct-mail campaign is of course, the letter. According to renowned marketing legend, Alan Rosenspan, research shows that the letter will account for 65-75% of the response rate.

While letters should include all the necessary information, go easy on your donors, alumni or clients. After all, the goal is not to have them read a long letter – it's for them to open their wallets! And if you're going to make a long letter, be sure to warn them the way Alan Rosenspan did.

Mr. Rosenspan wrote a direct-mailing piece for Geico Auto Insurance that was rather lengthy. To pique reader interest, he prefaced it with the following headline: *"No one wants to read a long ad about car insurance. So we made this a long ad about saving money."* As you can imagine, this brilliant direct-mailing paid for itself a thousand times over.

So whether your selling car insurance or selling a worthy cause, one thing is for certain – when it comes to successfully marketing your entity, the answer is always in the mail.

BOTTOM LINE ACTION STEP:
When sending out a direct mailing, make sure your communication is short, easy to read and intriguing enough to get opened.

3 CARDINAL RULES *for* DIRECT MAIL MARKETING

As we all know, raising money for non-profit organizations is always tough – all the more so in a shaky and turbulent economy. In tough economic times, non-profits are forced to review and reevaluate their fundraising strategies even more. I like to share a few general, simple and practical tips that can be applied to any organization's fundraising techniques – during good times and bad.

Rule number 1: Know your donors!

It is of paramount importance to create an effective marketing campaign with your donor in mind. For example, when launching a direct mailing, take care to start with an updated mailing list of donors. Wrong addresses, missed apartment numbers and misspelled names are all surefire ways to get your mailing ignored, misplaced or even thrown away.

As many in the marketing arena are aware, the key to any successful direct mail fundraising campaign is the letter. While writing the letter's copy, keep in mind that it's crucial to intrigue the reader. When marketing guru, Alan Rosenspan, was hired to do a direct mailing for American Express CreditAware (a company aimed at preventing identity theft), he emblazoned the letters with the following, eye-opening question: "How would you know if someone is using *your* name to open accounts?"

48

Not only were readers drawn into the letter's content, but many actually signed up for the American Express CreditAware program. Because in truth, whether you're selling credit card protection or trying to solicit funds, the primary goal of a direct mailing is to get your letter read. And a good way to guarantee that is by starting off with a provocative, eye-opening question.

Rule number 2: Make it interesting, tell a real story!

People would rather read a captivating story then a lengthy pitch. From a small organization with no money, to a large organization with many donors, presenting the letter in a story format will help ensure that recipients read your letter – and most importantly, donate to the cause.

The Wall Street Journal has been utilizing the story-in-a-letter format in their direct mail campaigns since 1974. According to the book, *Million Dollar Mailings,* this technique has been directly responsible for over $1 billion dollars in revenues for the Wall Street Journal since the campaign's inception.

Rule number 3: It's all in the writing!

Yeah, you're probably not going to believe this one, but it is true. The advertising agency of Ogilvy & Mather penned an intriguing direct mail piece for the Queen Elizabeth II World Cruise (arguably, the most famous cruise ship liner in the world) that was an astounding 13 pages long – and quite successful! While many are led to believe that when it comes to writing letters, the less text the better *("anything more than a page just won't get read!"),* high-quality writing – with the right mailing list to the to appropriate demographic – can prove otherwise.

Because after all is said and done, it's not always *how much* you write... it's *what* you write. (Obviously, take this with a grain of salt – don't send direct mail recipients a long letter unless a professional copywriter determines that it would be beneficial).

BOTTOM LINE ACTION STEP:

Communicating through direct mail is an effective way to get donors and business if it follows the cardinal rules.

EFFECTIVE TEASERS, HEADLINES & BOOK TITLES

David was a financial planner based in the Midwest with hundreds of satisfied clients. His company was launching a new investment opportunity and David wanted to inform existing clients of the news. He decided on a direct mail campaign and planned to enclose a letter detailing the benefits involved.

In order to attract their interest, David determined that it would be wise to offer clients free advice about the new investment – after all, who doesn't like something that's free? He needed a noticeable teaser to be stamped on the outer envelope – a powerful teaser that would grab the attention of the prospect and entice him to open the envelope.

Now stop for a moment. If you were David, what catchy line would you write to ensure that your envelope was opened?

Well, as any marketing professional will attest, there are two ways of doing it: the right way and the wrong way. Luckily, David enlisted the services of a marketing agency that created an effective teaser for him.

The teaser David came up with was: "Call for our FREE information!"

The marketing firm's teaser was: "Receive your FREE 12 page investing guide. Details inside."

See the difference?

The first one is a non-descriptive teaser that doesn't do much to describe the value of the offer or show why it's important. The other, however, packs a powerful punch, clearly illustrating how clients can receive valuable advice that could help them with their investments – at no cost whatsoever!

Lastly, by highlighting the number 12, the teaser showed a concrete figure that added a measure of trustworthiness to the offer – nothing ambiguous here! Through clearly detailing what the information was about and how it was relevant to the client, David ensured that his campaign was indeed a tremendous success.

A noted marketing expert once stated that, "It's all about the manner in which you present your offer – even more important than the actual offer itself!"

As an aside, many times I'm asked, "What books do you recommend on marketing?" Obviously there are many, but, I'll list some of my favorites below (and notice the power of an effective title – similar to the rules of effective teasers and headlines):

- **The 22 Immutable Laws of Branding:**
  How to Build a Product or Service into a World-Class Brand
  (Al Reis, Laura Reis)

- **Ogilvy on Advertising** (David Ogilvy)

- **The Tipping Point:**
  How Little Things Can Make a Big Difference (Malcolm Gladwell)

- **Differentiate or Die:**
  Survival in Our Era of Killer Competition (Jack Trout)

- **Guerrilla Marketing:**
  Easy and Inexpensive Strategies for Making Big Profits
  from Your Small Business (Jay Conrad Levinson)

- **The Sticking Point Solution:**
  9 Ways to Move Your Business from Stagnation to
  Stunning Growth In Tough Economic Times (Jay Abraham)

Notice how effective these titles are? The bottom line is, whether you're creating an envelope teaser, headline, brochure cover, book title, etc., make sure that the message or offer is clear. Although many factors determine the success of your marketing materials, a well-formulated message is clearly one of the most important factors in seeing effective results from your marketing efforts.

BOTTOM LINE ACTION STEP:

Make sure the message you are conveying in your communications are clear, accurate and detailed.

4 FOUR GOLDEN RULES *for* POWERFUL HEADLINES!

Henry S. Levy had a problem. The Brooklyn baker was having a difficult time selling his line of freshly baked rye bread products. His company was facing apathy from shoppers under the false impression that the Jewish-owned company's products were intended primarily for kosher consumers.

Mr. Levy knew that a powerful message had to be delivered to the public. A message that would generate interest and dispel the notion that his company was catering to only one specific demographic group. He enlisted the help of a young marketing whiz named Bill Bernbach to come up with a powerful ad campaign. Bernbach's mission would be to reach out to every segment of society and clearly illustrate why Levy's was indeed the choice rye bread for them.

A series of advertisements were created featuring a Navajo Indian, Irish cop and other ethnic characters chomping into thick rye sandwiches. The images were followed by the memorable and eye-catching headline: "You don't have to be Jewish to love Levy's real Jewish Rye."

The response that resulted propelled the Levy's brand into stardom, helped launch Bill Bernbach's career as an advertising prodigy, and has been lauded by Advertising Age as one of the most influential campaigns of the 20th century.

While there were many elements that contributed to the campaign's unprecedented success, the headline played a very major role. In a print ad, the headline's main purpose is to attract the attention of consumers and intrigue them into reading the rest of your advertisement.

According to the bestselling book, "Confessions of an Advertising Man," written by advertising legend David Ogilvy, five times as many people read the headline of an ad compared to the body copy (A.K.A. the text in the ad's middle describing the product or service). Therefore it's crucial that a headline jumps out at the reader and conveys a message that can be understood without having to read the entire ad from start to finish.

So the obvious question that begs to be asked is: How do I create ads with headlines that grab people's attention? The answer is: Keep on reading!

Listed below is what I like to call *"The 4 Golden Rules for Writing Powerful Headlines!"* They are based on the guidelines published by some of the most respected names in the industry including the aforementioned David Ogilvy and Bill Bernbach, and many agencies – including Bottom Line Marketing Group – have launched successful campaigns with these rules in mind.

Here goes!

Rule # 1: Use the right words!

- The words *"New"* and *"Free"* are undoubtedly from the most effective words in the English lexicon. For example, a headline trumpeting the words *"Brand New!"* has a much better chance of piquing the interest of consumers than a headline stating *"Recently Developed!"* Likewise, the word *"Free"* is probably the sweetest word a cash-strapped customer can hear. Need I say more?

Rule # 2: Give them a solution to their problems!

- Present consumers with a headline that solves whatever issues they may be encountering and they will absolutely want to find out more. Instead of writing a banal headline stating *"There Are Multiple Ways to Lose Weight"* why not grab people's attention with the curiosity-laden promise of *"The 9 Proven Ways to Shed Those Extra Pounds Now!"* In fact, you'll notice that the title of this essay is based directly on this premise – *"The 4 Golden Rules for Writing Powerful Headlines!"*

Rule # 3: Ask a question!

- A headline with an intriguing question never fails to capture people's attention. Geico had tremendous success sending out direct mailings with the following headline emblazoned on the envelope: "Are You Paying too Much for Car Insurance?" While it's not necessarily an earth-shattering or mind-boggling headline, it does get people thinking – and often gets them to open the envelope where they will read more about Geico's services.

Rule # 4: Let them say it for you!

- Using a client testimonial in a headline is a surefire way to add credibility to your sales message. When the U.S. School of Music launched a campaign touting music books that would teach users how to play musical instruments in a matter of weeks, copywriter John Caples created an unforgettable headline in the form of a testimonial: *"They Laughed When I Sat down At the Piano. But When I Started To Play..."* In essence, the headline was a riveting testimonial from a satisfied client who utilized the product to impress his disbelieving friends. Needless to say, the campaign was a tremendous success.

BOTTOM LINE ACTION STEP:

A powerful headline is essential. It will grab people's attention, get them reading, talking and buying!

OUT OF *the* BOX MARKETING

> " Some men look at things the way they are and ask why? I dream of things that are not and ask why not? "
>
> — *Robert Kennedy*

# BE DIFFERENT!

I'm often posed the same question: "What is one of the most important factors for launching a successful marketing campaign?" My answer: "Don't be afraid of being different!"

Some of America's most famous campaigns were wildly successful precisely because they dared to be different.

For example, the legendary Avis Rental Car advertising campaign from the 1960's highlighted the fact that they were only #2 in the rental car industry (Hertz was #1) and therefore had to go the extra mile when serving customers. True, it was a risky move to blatantly admit that they were not the biggest in the business, but Avis dared to be different... and they reaped the dividends.

Let's focus on the unique marketing campaign of a beverage that's very popular: Absolut Vodka!

Instead of following in the footsteps of other vodka companies and creating ads focusing on taste or flavor, Absolut broke the mold by launching a unique and award-winning campaign based on the product's distinct bottle shape, without mentioning anything about the vodka itself. Different? Yes. Successful? Absolutely (pun intended!).

In this spirit (yes, another silly pun!), here are a few ideas that can help you come up with a marketing campaign that dares to be out of the ordinary (a word to the wise: creating an out-of-the-box marketing campaign can be risky, so be sure to enlist the services of a reputable marketing agency for guidance).

According to an article in MediaPost, Liberty Tax Consultants – a large tax-preparation company with branches across the USA – has had much success by shedding its image of a stodgy CPA-type firm, thanks to its personal and slightly offbeat mascot: the male Statue of Liberty!

Each year around tax time, without fail, there are people dressed up in a Statue of Liberty costume, waving like maniacs to passing cars while pointing to the small Liberty Tax office nestled in the strip mall or store behind them. While it's not what a typical accounting agency would do to attract clients, it is quite effective and has generated tremendous exposure for the company (and you thought dressing up in a Statue of Liberty costume was just for kids!).

An airline company went with an extremely different and creative out of the box concept when it printed advertisements upside down to highlight its non-stop flights to Sydney, Australia (A.K.A. The Land Down Under – hence the upside down ad).

The bottom line? Lift up your cup of Absolut vodka, realize that a little craziness can generate huge results and make a toast to successful marketing!

BOTTOM LINE ACTION STEP:

Don't be afraid to be different. Create a zany out of this world advertising campaign that will grab attention...and results!

SMELLING the MONEY!

I would like to try an interactive exercise:

Find any newspaper (Wall Street Journal, New York Times, Washington Post, etc). Hold it firmly in both hands and slowly bring your nose toward the rectangular, ink-filled page.

Close your eyes and take a whiff.

What do you smell?

If it's a fresh newspaper copy, you may still be able to inhale the faint aroma of printing press ink.

Well get ready for the next marketing effect...thanks to revolutionary marketing technology, *"scented ink"* is soon coming to printing presses around the world.

As the name implies, "scented ink" is the new version of those Scratch & Sniff stickers from your childhood. Available in a variety of flavorful smells – including chocolate, popcorn, pickle and even cut grass – the popularity of combining advertisements, mailings and brochures with scented inks has been rising steadily.

According to an article in the industry magazine, Printing Impressions, one prominent non-profit organization achieved an astonishing 24% higher response rate by adding peppermint scented greeting cards to its fundraising package. Who would've thought that a little smell could generate such big results?

In fact, Louis Hau of Forbes Magazine notes that scented ink on a traditional print ad can sometimes provide better results than online ads. After all, you can't replicate a smell electronically – no matter how hard you scratch at the computer screen! The user-interaction created by scented inks will enable the consumer to remember your product or service long after the smell fades away.

But the key lesson here (from a marketing perspective) isn't necessarily the benefits offered by scented ink. Rather, it's the fact that successful businesses and organizations are continuously exploring ways of leveraging the latest marketing techniques – be it by e-marketing, rolling billboards, or scented ink – for maximum impact.

Of course, whether you're a non-profit organization or a for-profit corporation, you needn't necessarily use scented ink to promote your business message in a new way. Why not leverage something that's getting national media attention, like a NASA space satellite that's heading back to a crash landing on Earth?

One particular restaurant chain did just that a while back when a retired NASA satellite was scheduled to fall back on Earth somewhere in the Pacific Ocean. The restaurant placed a huge floating platform in the ocean with their logo in the middle – akin to an oversized dartboard – and announced that if the satellite landed squarely on the platform, everyone on planet Earth would get a free meal!

As you can imagine, the satellite didn't land anywhere near the platform – but the company landed on the front page of many newspapers nationwide! The publicity generated from this revolutionary marketing idea was tremendous. As were the profits.

In all, it is important for a successful entity to continue exploring the many new and different marketing solutions available to enhance growth, expansion and revenue. Keep in mind though, it would be wise to consult with an experienced marketing agency on how to make best use of the latest marketing tools available; especially if you embark on a radical marketing angle!

BOTTOM LINE ACTION STEP:

Creative marketing schemes will give your company publicity ... and profits.

A "MINER" LESSON
_in_ MARKETING

Remember back in 2010 when miners were trapped 2,300 feet below ground in Chile? Their amazing rescue serves as a valuable lesson in teamwork and perseverance, and it also presents a very unique lesson in marketing as well.

As everyone in the world vividly recalls, the accident occurred back in August of 2010, when the San José copper-gold mine, near Copiapó, Chile, collapsed, leaving 33 miners trapped deep below ground. After over 2 months of careful planning, the miners were finally shuttled up a narrow escape shaft to freedom, one miner at a time. The joyous reunions that took place each time a miner rose to the surface, followed the meticulously planned rescue operation, which ended the longest underground entrapment in human history.

What got my attention was the reaction of each rescued miner as they stepped foot onto the ground. Some stopped and prayed while others simply hugged their families and wept. But for one miner, Mario Sepulveda, the marketing spirit in him was on full display. The second of the 33 trapped Chilean miners to be rescued, he brought a bag of rocks with him from the underground cave as "souvenirs."

As rescuers chanted his name, he told the Chilean President Sebastian Pinera: "Wait a minute I have a present, here you go." He then handed over some rocks from the mine shaft, to laughs and cheers from the crowd. The president welcomed Mr. Sepulveda to the surfacing, adding: "Welcome back to your homeland."

The miner then walked over to the barricades and hugged and shook hands with the many workers who took part in the difficult rescue operation and cheered on elected officials before being taken to the field hospital for observation. The media immediately took to his winning personality and there was talk about him running for political office (where Bottom Line Marketing Group would be available to launch his political marketing campaign!).

The main lesson here is that the best way to get attention is by doing something out of the ordinary that grabs attention. Such as bringing up a bag of rocks from the mine. Or pressing the flesh with rescue workers in front of the cameras on the worldwide stage. While we will all eventually forget about the other 32 miners, we'll have a more difficult time forgetting the guy who had the spunk to bring up a bag of underground rocks as souvenirs for the crowd while undergoing a dangerous rescue attempt.

Of course you don't have to be a rescued miner to utilize the advantages of standing out and marketing yourself.

If you're a business creating an ad campaign, make it memorable, unusual or provocative using a few carefully chosen powerful words that stand out. Popular titles contain one or more of these words or phrases: *"Easy"; "The Secrets to..."; "Unlock"; "Insider"; "Time Sensitive"; "How to..."; "Free"; "Now You Can..."; "Discover"; and "Proven"*.

If you're sending out a direct mailing, stand out from the crowd by changing the typical look of your envelope into a unique shape that gets noticed. For example, an oversized full color or florescent colored envelope doesn't arrive in the mail box every day. It will get immediate attention and have a greater chance of being opened and read.

Additionally, the most conventional USA envelope size is #10. Try to shake things up a bit! By using a smaller #9 or taking advantage of the odd sized #12, you are marketing yourself differently than the other envelopes crammed into that mailbox and maximizing your return.

And if you own a store with a big front display window? When you create window displays that show small-scale items in a super-sized form, audiences are captivated and stunned by their dramatic appearance. Coffee cups, crayons, shoes, and guitars are all examples of typical small scale items that could be designed in a larger fashion and make your storefront look more appealing than the competition.

The bottom line? Don't be afraid to stand out from the crowd by doing things a little differently. And don't just take it from me – take a lesson from the clever miner who came up with a bagful of rocks...and wound up with a basket load of fame.

BOTTOM LINE ACTION STEP:
Be different and set yourself apart.

65

OF MANUSCRIPTS & MARKETING...

Recently at a "rare book" auction, an old and rare manuscript printed in Philadelphia in 1837 was auctioned off. Guess how much it went for? $47,000!

Sounds impressive, right? But get this: a month later, a similar manuscript at a used book shop in New England went for only a few hundred dollars!

What impresses me most, and explains the difference in price, is the venue where both of these manuscripts were sold.

When the posh auction house sold those manuscripts for nearly the purchase price of a brand new Lexus, everybody in attendance assumed that these books were of great value – even if the people didn't know the exact details behind these treasured books. The very fact that it was sitting on display in a bulletproof glass case at the auction house automatically spoke to the dealers and collectors gathered there and grabbed their attention.

Conversely, for the shoppers at the bookstore in New England who walked by that similar set of costly manuscripts, they were unable to appreciate the worth of those books sitting on a dusty shelf simply because it failed to speak to them. It was unable to grab their attention; the presentation, venue and atmosphere surrounding the book was just plain old wrong.

Which leads us to this topic.

While you may have the best company or business in the world, if you don't create and place your advertisements properly – and do not tailor your ad campaigns to the seasons, trends and even shopping preferences of the public – then the ad you are paying for will appear to be of no more value than those precious books simply piled on that book shop's shelf.

Here are a few different ad styles that can be used when launching a marketing campaign, and depending on your target market or product, can generate a successful response:

Business Card Ad – This type of ad cuts straight to the point by highlighting who you are, what you offer and where you're located. It always should include your logo and tag line. A business card ad will often generate the best response by running it year round. It keeps your name in front of potential consumers on a weekly basis and works especially well for service-based businesses such as plumbers, photographers and car services.

Coupon Ad – This form of advertising can prove to be an extremely successful sales promotion tactic by attracting new customers to your store or business.

By offering a specified dollar or percent amount off your merchandise or service, you will be giving potential clients a tangible incentive to give you the business. And once they do step foot in your door, you can impress them with what you've got to offer and get them to return again and again. Lastly, coupons are also one of the easiest ways to gauge ad effectiveness. Simply print the newspaper or magazine name alongside the coupon's edge and you'll have an instant database detailing which newspaper or magazine attracts the most customers.

Sale Ad – The only thing better than offering a discount to a particular customer? Offering a discounted sale to the entire world! Featuring a sale ad is akin to posting a formal invitation that invites the public into your store to receive a discount on a product, aisle or department. This particular advertising method works best during seasons such as around holidays, and of course, during the back-to-school season.

Spotlight Ad – This sort of ad focuses on a particular product, employee or customer of your business. It serves more to educate the public about a particular benefit you offer and can go a long way in helping establish your brand image. Another benefit is that it will help inform your client base about the nitty-gritty details that make your company or product so unique. However, if it's just educating the masses that you're after, check out the next advertising option listed below.

Informational Ad – The primary intention of this ad is to educate the public about your company or show the expertise you've acquired in your line of work. It could be written in a "Question & Answer" format offering professional advice or information. It could also be written in a journalistic style giving it the appearance of an article instead of an advertisement. And of course, diagrams or photo illustrations can be placed alongside the text of an informational ad giving readers the full scoop of what you're all about.

In all, when it comes to creating great ads, just think of *"The Tale of the Two Manuscripts"*...and you'll end up with a creative advertising campaign that's #1!

BOTTOM LINE ACTION STEP:

Presentation is everything!

Every advertiser's dream is to have a captive audience for his message, but finding folks to sit still for that message is more challenging than ever in our increasingly mobile and unfocused world. But some creative thinkers have been remarkably successful at finding a niche to get their message across without clutter or competition. You can too.

It would be a sweet dream indeed, since Osama bin Laden is 20,000 leagues under the sea and all, that just maybe, security can be relaxed for people flying at 35,000 feet. Anyone who has breathed a sigh of relief after passing through the pervasive airport security checks can relate to that.

One of the most annoying aspects of the security checks is when you have to take off your belt, shoes, hat, keys, coins, phone(s), coat and 72 other items into undersized bins, where at best, they get crushed and wrinkled, and at worst get mixed up with those of our fellow travelers.

Yet, Americans have this uncanny knack of making the most of adversity. Just ask Joe Ambrefe. Before we hear Joe's story, I want to thank my friend Mendy Hirth for bringing this item to my attention, and give thanks to a sharp CNN journalist, Bob Greene, for digging up a story when most fellow travelers were digging into clothing piles to find their shoes.

Stuck on line at Chicago's Midway International Airport, Greene grabbed a plastic bin to dutifully load his carry-on items for inspection. Something caught his attention as he was dropping his shoes in the bin: at the bottom of a bin was a colorful advertisement for an online merchant. To make sure he wasn't jet-lagged and seeing things, Greene examined a few other empty bins and, lo and behold, each one had a different ad laminated across the bottom of the bins.

"I found myself shaking my head in grudging admiration," wrote Greene. "While the rest of us were standing in those lines stewing over what the world has come to, one person among us saw a potential moneymaking opportunity just waiting to be snapped up."

This brings us back to Joe Ambrefe, founder and CEO of Florida's SecurityPoint Media. A frequent flyer, Joe figured out that passengers passing through security checks were a captive audience and that created an advertising opportunity!

Lest you think that pitching a product or service to surly people on airport security lines is a lost cause, major advertisers such as Sony, Microsoft, Honda, Charles Schwab, and even Amtrak have bought into Joe's idea. Their ads grace the bottoms of security bins in many of the major US airports.

Joe Ambrefe had it all figured out, and he even keeps the original napkin on which he wrote this idea, while waiting on line in an airport.

"Here is a contained area," Joe told CNN. "Air travelers are a very desirable demographic. It's a fantastic opportunity to speak to them." The advertisements in the plastic bins, he says, "can humanize the experience. They can put a smile on someone's face." Especially on Joe's face — for the money he's making off this idea. Besides owning the security bin concession at many airports, he recently told the St. Petersburg Times his goal is to add more airports in the coming months. Talk about flying high.

The lesson here for us is how advertising, broken down into its simplest component, is all about reaching your target market. Your message has to be captivating and it definitely helps to have a captive audience, but when it comes to placement, think out of the box and you might find cash tumbling into your bin!

BOTTOM LINE ACTION STEP:

Sometimes you can reach your target audience in the least likely of places. Keep a pen and a napkin (or iPad) handy for when the inspiration comes!

THE NAME OF *the* GAME

Keeping our good name is something we all strive for. After all, our names are synonymous with our reputations. In order to keep a name, we first have to devise one and that's when the creativity starts.

When it comes to naming newborns, the selection process is well established. Sometimes the baby is named after a departed loved one, sometimes after your favorite celebrity or character in a book, sometimes after someone in the Bible. Naming your business or other enterprise – is an equally great challenge. You only have one, or two, or three pithy words to tell people who you are and what you do.

How do marketers come up with the name? It's a great question. While professionals are trained for this, every time we are hired for a new job, it is a brand new contest.

The first step is to understand that choosing a name is a cooperative venture. Just as a husband and wife (hopefully) consult each other before naming their infant, I always ask my clients to suggest two names that they were already considering and to bring me two more that they already rejected. Hearing the client out and seeing their likes – and dislikes – clues me in as to how they think and what would best suit them.

Once the brainstorming process has begun, the marketing firm has to roll up its sleeves, do some market research on the potential names and apply plenty of creativity in figuring out which name will capture the market. A little more than 30 years ago, a company with humble beginnings in a garage began developing software for microcomputers. Its founder, Bill Gates, named the firm Microsoft. He named his business after what it did, but do you see how he made it catchy? (It's easier to walk up to the sales counter and say, I'd like to buy Microsoft Office, than I'd like to buy Software for Microcomputers Office.)

Now when Steve Jobs was stymied in naming his company, he threatened his creative team that if they didn't come up with a better name by 5 pm, he would name the company after his favorite fruit. Apple has little in common with computers, but boy what a bite they have taken out of the market. It just goes to show that there is more than one way to skin a cat (or peel an apple!) When it comes down to the Bottom Line (yes, I love the name), I am glad the idea popped into my head.

Yes, there are some time-honored approaches if you're stuck for a name. The Small Business Administration (SBA) suggests that you imagine how potential names will look on business cards, advertisements and with a logo. I would take this one step further these days, when every business must open along with an online presence. Since 98 percent of the English dictionary is already in use as URLs for websites, I advise proprietors to buy more than one prospective name. It only costs $10 a pop and that's a smaller price to pay than learning that the name you finally chose is no longer available.

The SBA also recommends making sure the name is easy to pronounce and to be careful about its connotations. That's where a good marketing firm comes into play again, because we are trained to spot nuances.

BOTTOM LINE ACTION STEP:
When drawing up the plans for a new business,
"Crown it with a good name!"

BREATHING LIFE
into **IDEAS**

Some ideas we might think of, can lead to great inventions, while others might simply "crash and burn." Yet, all ideas are worthy of at least some discussion. The only bad ideas are the ones we hesitate to bring up.

It has been known to happen. A board of directors or organizational volunteers meets to kick around ideas to boost revenues or fundraising. One participant recommends sending out a newsletter or a direct mail piece. Another participant dismisses the idea on the spot, saying something to the effect of, whenever I get a brochure in the mailbox it goes straight to the trash can unopened, so why should we spend our money on that.

This reaction can come from even the most decent people who have only the best interests of the organization at heart. However, there is a facet of human nature that contains an initial, knee-jerk reaction to kill an idea, or to be dismissive without giving the matter its due consideration.

When I hear a story of this nature, I recall the famous quote from a great rabbi, Noach Weinberg, who built an empire of educational institutions from scratch. He said, "When you start something new, everybody says you're crazy. When you're halfway successful they say:

I knew it all along. You know when you're really successful? When they say: I can do it better than you."

Successful people know that the naysayers are often reflecting their own weaknesses, or lack pro-activity or inspiration. This needs to be handled on a few levels, the first of which is to treat it as any objection to the sales process, and objections are made to be overcome.

So if someone remarks that brochures end up in trash bin, (if it's worth your time) it might pay to ask that person if he ever received a piece of unsolicited mail that he opened, and if so, what grabbed his attention? Or if someone objects saying we don't have the budget to produce sales or fundraising literature, you might counter by saying, let's say budget was no factor, how would you recommend we promote our new product or program?

On a different level, the idea-presenter must ensure that the idea is well-thought out. It is best to iron out the kinks and find solutions to possible objections before formally presenting it to your board by discussing it first with those who you would trust to execute it. That way, if objections arise in the meeting, you have an ally who will speak up on your behalf.

Also, the more effort you invest in planning ahead, the wiser use you will be making of your and committee members valuable time. *Know-How Non-Profit*, a project of the Cass Centre for Charity Effectiveness in London, recommends putting thought into whom you invite, the environment, and the time of day (or night) when the meeting will be held. Then, make it clear that the ground rules of the meeting will be to use a range of creative thinking techniques under the banner of listening and building on others' ideas, anything is possible, and then have fun and go all out.

Now, you may ask, what happens if I am attending such a meeting and I hear an idea that I truly and legitimately feel is not right for our organization or company. Don't I have an obligation to speak up?

This is indeed a fair and honest question. In her book *Creativity in Business: A Practical Guide for Creative Thinking,* Dr. Carol Kinsey Goman answers that the best way to phrase such sentiment is in a straightforward manner, such as: "Here are some concerns that I have. Could you help me to understand how they would be overcome?"

By directing the situation back to the person who proposed the idea in a diplomatic and positive fashion, you allow that person to develop a response to your concerns, while still keeping the door open to further discussion that could hone the idea and turn it into a real winner for everyone.

BOTTOM LINE ACTION STEP:
Be known as an 'idea creator' not an 'idea killer.'

GREAT SLOGANS & TAGLINES

The American Nation is built upon a culture of phrases, slogans and tag lines.

From the scientific ("That's one small step for man...") to the political ("Yes We Can!") to the tragic ("Remember the Alamo!"), these memorable slogans serve their purpose as easy-to-recall nuggets of information; a form of media that encapsulates large messages with short bursts of words.

But without a doubt, the most memorable slogans come from – where else? The advertising and marketing industry.

Think about it. You jump out of your mattress that you bought from Sleepy's ("For the rest of your life"), turn on your bedroom light ("GE – We bring good things to life!"), gargle and rinse your mouth out with Listerine mouthwash ("The taste you hate twice a day!").

You then brush your teeth with Crest toothpaste ("Look ma, no cavities!"), put on your Lenscrafter glasses ("Glasses in less than an hour!"), eat a quick breakfast of Rice Krispies ("Snap, crackle and pop!")

and open the Yellow Pages to call the plumber ("Let your fingers do the walking!") because your kitchen sink ("The bold look of Kohler") is backed up thanks to your toddler having stuffed his brand new toy down the drain ("I'm a Toys R Us kid!").

In all, every single part of your day has a popular, well-known slogan that can be applied to it.

As you can see, it is extremely important for every company to have a catchy, memorable phrase that sums up its mission and message. Let us point out some of the underlying points behind the above slogans to give you a better understanding of why slogans work – and how you can go about making a successful catchphrase for your own company.

According to an article in Advertising Age, there are some important characteristics that all successful slogans share:

First, the slogans must be brief. Because the truth is, everybody can remember a quick jingle or catchy phrase – but most people can't remember long essays or lengthy chapters from an encyclopedia. So when it comes to creating a winning slogan, less is definitely more!

Furthermore, the slogans should not be too funny or extremely clever. Consumers come in all shapes, sizes and IQs. A slogan that sounds more like a geometry equation and less like a sales pitch won't be too effective. A slogan's purpose is to convey a powerful message – not the commercial equivalent of a knock-knock joke.

Many famous slogans highlight a specific characteristic about the product. For example, the Sleepy's slogan quoted above is quite straightforward and allows people to visualize a good night's sleep, while purchasing a product that will last for a long time.

The words of every successful slogan must flow easily. Crest's legendary slogan of "Look ma, no cavities" is so simple that it can be uttered by even the smallest of children. Likewise, who doesn't appreciate the beauty of the Rice Krispies cereal slogan? One whose words aren't even a genuine part of the English language, but rather made up of the actual sound the product makes. Snap, crackle and pop anyone?

If you're creating a slogan for a large company, keep in mind your many employees as well. GE (General Electric) has a slogan that most certainly evokes pride in the workplace and serves to enhance employee morale. After all, who doesn't want to be part of a company that's "Bringing good things to life"? Additionally, according to Advertising Age, GE's investors and shareholders benefit from the slogan as well. It instills in them a sense of confidence in the company, because constantly "bringing good things to life" translates into the fact that GE is constantly creating new products – and therefore generating further revenue.

So, as you embark upon creating a defining slogan for your company – after you downed your morning Maxwell House coffee ("Good to the last drop!") – contact a marketing agency to sum up your company in a powerful one liner. Hopefully, they'll "hit the nail on the head!"

BOTTOM LINE ACTION STEP:
Create a slogan that everyone can understand and relate to.

NAMING *your* COMPANY

Looking to make serious money? Forget about real estate, insurance and mortgages – instead, focus on naming babies! According to an article in the Wall Street Journal, an entirely new industry of professional baby-naming consultants are billing parents-to-be with hefty fees to come up with unique, inimitable and relevant baby names.

In fact, a company called Baby Names began offering half-hour name consulting sessions by phone for the discounted price of – only $95. They also boast a website that sells lists of customized names for $35. As of this writing, their website receives well over a million visitors per month!

It goes to show that names are sometimes worth spending money on – particularly when it's a business name.

The name of a company must evoke something. It can be an image. A specific message. Or even just plain old curiosity. But it's more than something to identify your business with. A name can enhance your corporate image, broaden your marketing horizons and generate tremendous exposure for your entity.

So, now you're probably wondering how a company should go about deciding on a name. Well, here are a few proven tips that can most certainly make the name-selection process easier.

Firstly, avoid settling on names that are too restrictive and binding. For example, if a retail cellular phone store were to call itself 'New Jersey Cellular', it may very well end up possessing a loyal customer base in the Garden State – but it would probably have a hard time expanding and branching into other demographic regions. After all, why would somebody in Delaware purchase a phone from a store dubbed 'New Jersey'?

Keep in mind though, that having a specific name can be advantageous if the product can benefit from the image it will evoke. A pizza store in Florida would be attracting potential customers by giving itself the title of 'New York Pizza', a marketing technique known as "foreign branding." It reminds me of the Pizza store in Jerusalem called "Manhattan Pizza," and the Pizza store in Manhattan called "Jerusalem Pizza!" Same goes for an upscale watch store calling itself 'The Swiss Timepiece' and effectively riding on the marketing coattails of the term 'Swiss' – a phrase that has become synonymous with accuracy and quality.

Another popular option when naming a business is blending multiple words together into a memorable name. The benefits are twofold: First, chances are nobody else will have that particular name, allowing your entity to gain immediate and instant recognition. Naturally, you'll benefit if the name can sum up the premise of your business, allowing clients to immediately realize exactly what your company does – before they even read your brochure or visit your website.

S.B. Master, the noted naming consultant, tells of how an Italian vacation and touring company came to him seeking a unique name. Settling on a decisively simple name, Master came up with the wildly successful, 'Italiatour', conjuring up the perfect image of "Italy' and 'Tour' with an imaginary name not even found in the dictionary.

While some entrepreneurs prefer to actually make up names that have no inherent meaning, professional marketers generally agree that it's only a good idea if the entrepreneur has the resources and time to educate potential customers about what the name stands for. Take Microsoft, Google or Yahoo for example – all invested significant marketing dollars to promote and educate the world what the company does.

For instance, legendary ice cream company Haagen Dazs was actually founded by a Jewish couple named Reuben and Rose Mattus in 1961. However, to reinforce their ice cream products with an upscale image, they settled on the made up name of 'Haagen Dazs' – words that sound Scandinavian but have no actual meaning in any language.

This phenomenon is known within the marketing industry as 'foreign branding', which basically involves using a foreign-sounding name to imply the superiority of a particular product. A prominent example of this concept would be upscale home-appliance company Haier, whose name evokes an image of European precision.

Lastly, it's important to work hand-in-hand with your marketing agency and ensure your company's name, logo and corporate identity all jive well. A trendy-sounding business name with a staid, serious logo will give consumers a mixed message about your company and quite possibly confuse them. Make sure that every element of your identity clearly relates to one another. And finally, don't forget to make sure that the new name is available as a "dot.com" domain.

Because at the day's end, it's about more than just a company name... it's about your company's future as well.

BOTTOM LINE ACTION STEP:
The name is the first step in your company's identity and success.

EXECUTION

> *In the modern world of business, it is useless to be a creative original thinker, unless you can also sell what you create. Management cannot be expected to recognize a good idea, unless it is presented to them by a good salesman.*
>
> — *David M. Ogilvy*

DO MARKETERS LIVE IN _the_ ZOO?

Do you know what a guerilla is?

No, not those big hairy things that eat bananas and live in the zoo. I am referring to the term used for describing someone who fights an enemy with unconventional tactics. Typically used during times of war, the term guerilla can also connote a businessperson who maneuvers successfully his way across the corporate battlefield thanks to creativity, cleverness and ingenuity.

In the advertising and marketing industry, there is an expression called "Guerilla Marketing." Coined and used as a book title by legendary marketing guru, Jay Conrad Levinson, it is used to describe a marketer that doesn't go with the flow, but rather discovers previously unrecognized marketing opportunities.

But contrary to popular belief, the basic tenets of guerrilla marketing are not complex – they're actually deceivingly simple. They just require a little forethought and planning.

For example, many unwitting businesspeople believe in the famous expression, "Sell the sizzle not the steak." As a guerilla marketer, you will immediately realize that the only way to successfully advertise your business is by selling neither the sizzle nor the steak – it's by selling a solution!

Because, according to Mr. Levinson in his best-selling book, the easiest way to sell anything is to position it as a solution to a problem. While the sizzle is nice and all (and may even stay in their minds for a long time after they've seen your ad), it won't necessarily get a prospective customer to actually purchase your product or use your service. However, if you offer them a realistic solution to a realistic problem, they will be almost guaranteed to take an interest in your solution.

Case in point: In the 1950's, many drug companies were manufacturing aspirin-type products that were intended to relieve headaches and pains. The majority of these companies created ads focusing on the pureness of ingredients, experience of the particular company, or how it was simply effective at taking away minor aches and pain.

One drug company, Anacin, came to the conclusion that simply following the pack and touting the same old sales pitch wasn't going to give them an edge over the competition. They recognized that something different – a Unique Selling Proposition (known within the marketing industry as a USP) – would be required to give the brand a much-needed boost. The renowned Ted Bates & Co. advertising agency was hired to launch an extensive advertising campaign for Anacin at a cost of many millions of dollars.

The memorable advertising campaign played on a typical consumer's feelings by focusing neither on the cleanliness of ingredients nor on corporate experience. Because after all, when a client is in pain with a terrible headache, he is not thinking about these trivialities. Rather, he's thinking just one thing – "Get rid of this headache quickly!"

Hence the advertising line that became famous worldwide: "Anacin provides relief fast, fast, fast!"

While the other drug companies were busy selling the sizzle and the steak (or at the very least, attempting to), Anacin was busy selling the solution. And as you can imagine, consumers became intrigued by the product that promised to relieve pain rapidly and the company began turning a tremendous profit...fast, fast, fast!

True, critics of the Anacin campaign have lamented that the drug company didn't actually do anything to distinguish its product's significant advantages; but many in the industry believe that it didn't make much of a difference. The goal of any advertising campaign is to successfully advertise a product and ensure the client makes a profit. Which in the case of Anacin and Ted Bates & Co., it did.

So when it comes to marketing your product or service, be sure to keep the sizzling steaks in the oven where they belong – and be sure to leave the advertising solutions in the hands of the professionals who will help ensure your company rises to the top... fast, fast, fast!

BOTTOM LINE ACTION STEP:

Execute your marketing campaign by selling your product as the solution to their problem.

MARKETING TAKEN TO THE CLEANERS, *Part I*

Want to brush up on your geography, social studies and marketing skills? Your best bet is to head over to your local dry cleaners! At least that's what I do. Who knew that picking up a pair of freshly laundered pants would be such an eye-opening experience?

But let's start from the beginning.

Like most other working professionals, my standard corporate attire includes a starched shirt and pressed pants that are laundered by a dry cleaners in my neighborhood. Aside from dodging meter maids and maneuvering past labyrinths of double-parked cars, going there is usually an uneventful experience. However, one week proved otherwise.

Upon picking up my weekly order from the cleaners on Friday afternoon, I was suddenly struck by the plastic covering hanging over my pleated pants. Emblazoned boldly on the plastic was an advertisement. Now advertising on dry cleaning paraphernalia is nothing new – it's been around for years and is actually a good way to advertise a local business within a defined neighborhood or district.

But this wasn't your typical ad for a supermarket, clothing store or gift shop. Rather, it was an ad (are you ready for this one?) from the

Korean Government! The headline ad proclaimed "Dokdo Island is Korean Territory." The body copy read: "For the last 2,000 years, the body of water between Korea and Japan has been called the 'East Sea.' Dokdo (two islands) located in the East Sea is part of Korean territory. The Japanese government must acknowledge this fact."

Um, OK. I mean yes sir! Actually as I was standing there in middle of the cleaners, I started laughing in amazement at the absurdity of this advertising attempt. Let's get this straight: the Korean government was advertising to me to support their side in a diplomatic disagreement that they're currently having with Japan.

I mean, here I am, born and raised in New York, living in New York, running a business in New York and driving a car with New York license plates. Do I look like someone who is involved in the world of Korean and Japanese politics? Don't get me wrong, I'm honored to be well known and well respected in my field and my community, but I'm not the Secretary of State! The closest connection I have to anything on that side of the planet is my occasional order of General Tso's Chicken placed at a local Kosher Chinese takeout (which may land me back at the cleaners for some size adjustments...).

While I don't know who the agency behind this was or why they chose a predominantly Jewish section of Brooklyn as a targeted segment for this campaign, something tells me that this is a severe case of demographics going awry. "Demographics?" you may ask. "Isn't that the name of a designer shirt?" Well no, not quite.

Demographics – used extensively within the advertising and marketing industry – are the studying and analyses of specific populations or marketplaces. As every marketing professional will agree, demographics are crucial to the success of an advertising campaign.

Proper demographic data would guarantee, for example, that ads for dentures don't appear in a magazine read mostly by children – or that ads geared toward people of Asian ethnicity don't end up in a dry cleaning store frequented primarily by Jews in Brooklyn, New York.

Because at the day's end, accurate demographic research ensures that ads being launched in a campaign are geared toward and will be seen by their proper target markets.

Now somewhere within the cogs of the aforementioned dry cleaners bag's advertising campaign, something got mixed up. Perhaps it was due to oversight that caused a client to spend unnecessary time and money on a campaign that possibly never reached its target market.

I can just imagine the conversation that went on between the ad agency boss and his employee. It probably went something like this:

> **Boss:** *We need some demographic data for the Korean government's ad campaign. Any good ideas?*
>
> **Employee:** *Yeah! Lots of dry cleaners are owned by Asians. Let's slap the ads on the side of their plastic bags and we'll easily get the message across!*
>
> **Boss:** *Great idea! Splendid! I think someone here deserves a raise.*
>
> **Employee:** *Why thank you!*
>
> **Boss:** *No, I'm referring to myself. I'm giving myself a raise for being so smart and hiring you.*
>
> **Employee:** *Oh.*

While the above conversation is mostly imagined, it does illustrate the importance of doing proper demographic research before launching a campaign.

BOTTOM LINE ACTION STEP:

Before you execute your campaign, make sure all your research is done – especially your market research and demographic studies.

MARKETING TAKEN TO THE CLEANERS, *Part II*

Is it totally hilarious that a foreign government would launch an expensive marketing campaign targeted at Asians... in a predominantly Jewish area?

Truthfully speaking, it really wasn't such a bad idea (except that the targeting was off by a couple of zip codes!) Had the campaign been launched in a targeted demographic zone such as the Chinatown district or around the United Nations compound in New York City, it may have actually accomplished the intended campaign goals. The method used for the campaign was quite clever; it was the targeting and placement aspect that caused things to become discombobulated.

Let us focus on the actual advertising method and see how it could have successfully been implemented:

Mr. Feng Zhāng of Chinatown goes to the local dry cleaners and picks up his pants. He sees the advertisement on the cleaners bag and nods knowingly, fully aware of the issue between the Korean and Japanese governments.

He then goes next door to the shoemaker and waits in line to pick up his shoes. Behind Mr. Zhāng stand several people waiting in line impatiently. The ad catches their attention and they too immediately realize what the message is about.

Mr. Zhāng then carries the bag to his house located a few blocks away. Along the route, dozens of passerby see the cleaners' bag and immediately understand the significance of the advertisement. In essence, the advertisement is serving as a typical print ad for Mr. Zhāng, banner ad for the people at the shoemaker, and walking billboard for the passerby on the street. Talk about bang-for-the-buck!

By the time Mr. Zhāng walks through his front door, dozens of people – all who know of the situation – will have seen the ad and possibly been influenced by it. Bingo!

A typical example of how an unconventional advertising method can generate a huge response.

But of course, we can learn from the above illustration and apply it to your business as well. Here are 3 ideas – at very little additional cost since they leverage existing tools – that can serve as powerful marketing-boosters for your business:

- **Turn every outgoing piece of paper into a mini-ad!**

  Whether it's your business card, stationary or simply an invoice, spice it up with a unique message or fact about your company. Don't just print your telephone number and address on your envelopes or receipts – be sure to tack on a memorable slogan, brief testimonial from a client, or a photo of your corporate headquarters. In essence, don't view the envelope as a device that's used for mailing things – view it as a portable print ad that will be prominently displayed, courtesy of the United States Postal Service! Likewise, don't let the back of your business card get lonely – put an important fact or some bullet points on those 3.5 x 2 inches of blank white space. Believe it or not, people will see it, read it and most importantly, remember it!

- **Transform your vehicle into a rolling billboard!**

  Walking along any main street or thoroughfare are thousands of people who can be your potential clients. The very least you can do is let them know your company is there to serve them! While it goes without saying that every truck or delivery van should have a full-color display on its side, the same rings true for the family minivan – especially if it's used at times for business purposes. Magnetic decal signs can be placed on its sides, transforming it from an ordinary family car into an extraordinary rolling advertisement! Of course, when the situation warrants, those signs can be easily removed, allowing your personal 'ad-mobile' to once again perform carpool duty discreetly.

- **Freebies, freebies and more freebies!**

  Everybody loves a freebie! Whether it's a pen, calendar or magnet, a complimentary item with your company name on it is always appreciated – and if useful – will certainly be used. In fact, if you can find a creative and memorable freebie that jives with your particular industry or business, all the better! For example, the Philadelphia Cream Cheese Company launched a marketing campaign that involved giving out free cream cheese storage containers. Every time clients would open their fridge doors and look inside, the container – proudly bearing the Philadelphia Cream Cheese logo – would stare back at them, effectively keeping the company's image and product in clients' minds.

BOTTOM LINE ACTION STEP:
Leverage all marketing materials to get your message out.

COLOR WAR
for BUSINESSES

Does the following scenario sound familiar?

You're driving to an important business meeting and running slightly behind schedule. The road looks relatively empty, so you gun the engine up a notch, nudge the odometer needle a bit higher and shift into overdrive. And then it happens.

The roar of your trusty V6 is overpowered by a piercing, whiny noise – the siren of a police car. We all know what happens next. "Yes officer, no officer, I'm sorry officer...see you in traffic court officer." But it really doesn't have to be that way. The fact is, some people have a higher chance of getting pulled over and slapped with hefty speeding tickets than others.

According to a study performed in New Zealand and published in the British Medical Journal, drivers operating red-colored vehicles are 16% more likely to get pulled over than those driving cars with neutral colors. While that statistic may come as a surprise to you, for those in the marketing business, it's a no-brainer.

Colors have always played a crucial role in the advertising and marketing process. From portraying a product as trustworthy to creating an image of quality, the design and color-scheme surrounding a brand can absolutely make it or break it.

For example, the aforementioned color of red is a powerful one that serves to grab the attention of people and exudes a feeling of power, action and adrenaline. Therefore, a red car racing by a police officer is more likely to be noticed than a gray one. Likewise, a toy product packaged in a bright red box is more likely to catch the attention of a young child than a dull brown package.

But the color red is more than just an attention grabber – according to consumer psychologists, red stimulates the appetite (as does its cousin, orange). If you are in the restaurant or food business, be sure to have the color red as part of your décor, logo and color scheme... it can certainly prove to stimulate your bank account!

Alternatively, the color blue is known to be a relaxing, calming color that is used by chromotherapy specialists to help people lose weight, as the color blue has been proven to slow the metabolism. Come to think of it, perhaps that's why there aren't any foods that are naturally colored blue (true, there are blueberries, but they really are bordering on purple). However, blue is used extensively by spas, beauty clinics and industries where relaxation or therapy is utilized, along with travel agencies and vacation clinics (think bright blue skies, rich blue seas and so on).

Blue's neighbor on the color wheel, green, evokes a feeling of trustworthiness and responsibility. Ever wonder why the paper currency of our country is green? Chances are, it wasn't because Staples had a sale on green ink toner. Likewise, many prominent financial firms boast logos with green undertones that serve to reassure and encourage clients.

Green in a slightly lighter shade also connotes an impression of nature, rejuvenation and freshness. Many organic, macrobiotic and health food products incorporate green into their packaging. As of late, the color green has also become associated with ecological and environmental awareness, symbolizing a message of renewal.

White is the color that represents – what else? – purity. Skin care products, low-fat foods and companies in the pharmaceutical sector can benefit from using the color white in their marketing efforts to convey a message of wholesomeness and cleanliness.

While the color black has traditionally been viewed as a negative color, it too – when used properly – can convey an image of quality and superiority. For example, when Coca-Cola's orange juice brand, Minute Maid, entered the cluttered juice market, it avoided the typical green and orange color motifs used by existing companies such as Tropicana and Grower's Choice. Rather, it settled on an impressive color scheme of black and orange, positioning itself as a premium orange juice company. Judging from the immediate response and subsequent success it has encountered, the strategy paid off quite handsomely.

In fact, Coca-Cola and Pepsi make tremendous use of colors in their feuding media campaigns designed to attract customers. While some in the industry have dubbed the ongoing battle "The Cola Wars," I respectfully suggest a more appropriate moniker: "The Color Wars."

Because the reality is, colors do more than just enhance a business's logo or product's packaging – colors can generate tremendous profits as well. Hopefully, we will get to see that green!

BOTTOM LINE ACTION STEP:
Proper use of color can greatly affect the positioning of your product.

 # MULTI-CHANNEL MARKETING

Ahh, minivans. If you are a parent of young children, chances are you currently own – or will eventually purchase – a minivan. Capable of seating large families, noisy toddlers and frazzled parents, the amenities offered by minivans have become an integral part of everything from family trips to shopping excursions – and of course, carpool (A.K.A. Mom's Taxi)!

Without a doubt, the most distinctive part of a minivan isn't the optional third-row cup holders – it's the sheer amount of entry and exit space. Large front doors allow moms to climb into the driver's seat wielding an oversized purse on one arm and a Carter's diaper bag dangling from the other. Voluminous side doors enable growth-spurting youngsters to scramble into the back row alongside cookie-munching toddlers. And a gargantuan rear hatch easily swallows up bulky double-strollers, giant suitcases and piles of hefty suit bags.

The minivan proves to be a veritable lesson in automobile engineering – and marketing too!

Think about it: successful companies, businesses and organizations generally utilize multiple ways to market their entities. A print advertisement in a newspaper is a particularly effective medium in spreading your message to the masses. However, a newspaper ad *together* with a direct mail campaign will generate a much higher response and draw a wider audience – much like the minivan that utilizes multiple doors and hatches to enable easier access for teens, babies and suitcases. In addition to ads and mailings, throw in a website banner that links to your company's website, and radio spots, and you've got a serious, wide-reaching marketing campaign underway.

Legendary marketing guru Jay Conrad Levinson sums up this concept well in his bestselling book, "Guerilla Marketing."

"Guerilla marketers know that *marketing combinations* work," he writes. "If you run a series of ads, have a website, and then do a direct mailing or e-mailing, they'll all work, and they'll each help each other work. We're living in an era where marketing combinations open the doors to marketing success."

Within the industry, this phenomenon is called *multi-channel marketing* (not to be confused with multi-level marketing). Simply put, multiple marketing channels reinforce your business message in the minds of your clients and prospects. Retailers have leveraged the advantages of multi-channel marketing in many ways. Here are some additional "low cost" methods that you can put to use for *your* business:

- Industry statistics show that 70% of all business calls are placed on hold for approximately a minute. That, in essence, adds up to thousands of free advertising minutes per year. Instead of piping Beethoven's Ninth Symphony across the phone lines, why not direct clients waiting on hold to visit your website where they can take advantage of money-saving offers? Or use those precious minutes to inform them about your upcoming sales and promotions. A few short minutes of on-hold advertising can generate some very tall profits.

- Business cards can hold more than just information. One restaurant owner that I know of hands out business cards with a printed offer on the back that states: *Present this card for a complimentary dessert.* This unique sales pitch has drawn an untold amount of customers to his eatery and generated tremendous word-of-mouth publicity.

- Invite potential customers to visit your website where they can print out valuable money-saving coupons. Dozens of name-brand retails stores such as Lord & Taylor, Macy's and GAP attract customers with this method – why not follow in their footsteps and start increasing the foot traffic in your place of business?

- Some companies spend six-digit figures to have their messages plastered across large billboards. For many industries (notably for autos), that happens to be a particularly effective medium. However, if your business has a delivery van or truck (or minivan!) why not transform it into a low-cost rolling billboard, replete with eye-catching colors and graphics? And when it's not being driven on the road, be sure to park the vehicle in a high-profile area where passerby will notice it – and your business message too!

The effects of multi-channel marketing are powerful and will help you meet your business sales goals – to attract both new clientele and re-enforce your positioning with current clients.

BOTTOM LINE ACTION STEP:
Use a variety of mediums in order to help get your message across.

 HOW MUCH SHOULD YOU BUDGET *for* MARKETING?

Do you like solving riddles? Alright, here's one: If an American Airlines flight flew from New York to Ohio (a distance of 402 miles, via air travel) and required 1,842 gallons of gas to complete the trip, how many gallons of gas would a Delta Airlines flight flying from New York to California (a distance of 2,451 miles) require?

Stumped? Well, to be honest there is no exact answer. As any pilot can attest, every flight poses its own challenges. The precise amount of gasoline needed fluctuates based on an airplane's altitude, flight direction and even surrounding weather conditions. Before taking off, pilots will take all these variables into account and ensure there's enough gasoline for the plane to reach its final destination.

Now you don't necessarily need to be a pilot to appreciate this answer. For those in the marketing industry, this situation sounds all too common.

Often, a potential client will ask the following question: "How much will a marketing campaign cost me?"

My usual response will actually be a variety of questions, such as: "What are your goals? How much do you want to increase sales by? How many new clients do you want? Which new markets are you entering? How much market share do you wish to capture?" In essence, it all depends on their vision.

Because the reality is, every marketing campaign has to begin with a vision and goal. Akin to the pilot who must determine where he wants to fly to before taking off, businesses and organizations too, must take into account who they are trying to reach and what they're endeavoring to accomplish before attempting to "fly" toward their targets.

Confused? Okay, here's an example: If a non-profit organization's goal is to create a simple direct-mail campaign to solicit via technical fundraising, a modest budget will be sufficient. However, if that same organization's goals were to fundraise nationally, it would require an intensive campaign targeting areas with large demographics. Additionally, it would involve launching multiple advertisements, segmented direct-mail packages and a hi-tech website, to name just a few. The goal and the return are much higher in the latter case, thus requiring a higher budget.

An analogy would be, that the brochure for the Toyota Camry, although impressive, is noticeably simpler than an upscale version created for the Lexus LS!

A simple trifold brochure is sufficient for many projects. However, if you need to make an impression on a big-ticket item – or looking to impress a prospective donor for a major contribution – you'll need an upscale brochure to make the right impact. Again, the budget is determined by your goals and visions.

Here are a few important points to keep in mind when creating a campaign – aspects that will directly influence the cost and success of your project:

KNOW YOUR TARGET MARKET:

Define the target markets you are attempting to reach. For instance, if you are a mortgage company trying to reach first-time home buyers, don't simply advertise your message to every person on the planet. Avoid waste by focusing exclusively on the 25-35 year old crowd – a demographic group that belongs in that category. In other words, help identify your campaign's goals – and its budget – by clearly knowing who your target markets are.

CREATE METHODS OF COMMUNICATION:

What methods will your company use to spread its message? Running radio ads for a year straight isn't the only way to get your name out there. Discussing alternative marketing ideas with your agency can prove quite advantageous. Tap into the power of media advertising, brochures, e-mail marketing, posters, social media, internet banner ads, etc. Clearly delineate how you want to reach potential markets... and your going after them will be a whole lot easier!

FOCUS ON MICRO-TARGETING:

Knowing how big of an audience you have will drastically influence the campaign's budget. If you are only focusing on marketing to one particular community, then utilize local media to spread the message. Take a local newspaper for example. Any upcoming event that will be occurring in Staten Island is generally advertised in – where else? – the Staten Island Advance. Advertisers are guaranteed that Staten Island residents reading the Advance will most certainly see their ads and be informed (and you thought guarantees were only for Bugaboos!).

TAKE CHARGE OF YOUR COMPANY'S IMAGE!
How does the public perceive your company or organization? Spending money on promotions or events that don't clearly relate to your business' message can prove to damage more than just your wallet – it can blur your entity's image as well. Every campaign (in addition to focusing on monetary goals) should aim to enhance a company's overall image and increase its future brand value as well.

In all, planning and goals aren't just for airplane pilots – they're for you too! Be sure to create successful marketing goals that will accurately guide your business or organization's marketing campaign... and, like an airplane, your profits will soar!

BOTTOM LINE ACTION STEP:
Assign a marketing budget in proportion to your vision.

STAMP *an* IMPRESSION

Some nations generate revenue by exporting food products or electronics – others, with automobiles or oil. And for a select few, profits are produced with postage stamps.

Postage stamps!?

Yes, those colorful paper stamps pasted on envelope corners are actually tremendous cash-cows for certain foreign countries. You see, stamp collectors are always looking for elaborate postage stamps and limited edition prints. So these countries continuously print limited runs of unique, different and colorful collector's edition stamps to feed the masses of collectors looking for exclusive finds.

As the matter of fact, according to Wikipedia, the stamps produced by these countries far exceed their inhabitant's postal needs. But that's alright – the stamp collectors are there to snatch up (and pay top-dollar for) the leftovers. Due to this trend, the annual world output averages about 10,000 different stamp types per year.

Sounds impressive? Perhaps. But here's what's even more impressive: you too can generate tremendous profits by utilizing the benefits of postage stamps.

No, you don't have to be a third-world country printing limited editions of colorful stamps adorned with dancing elephants. All you've got to do is think like a first-rate marketer – and use the power of stamps to sell your message via direct mail.

How? Firstly, while the letter and envelope of a direct mailer are extremely important, don't forget about the type of stamp on the mailing's front. Marketing personality, Alan Sharpe, recommends using commemorative stamps that will make your mailing stand out amongst the standard "Forever" stamps and corporate-looking metered postage envelopes.

But you are not limited to using only one stamp. A combination of two, three or even four different postage stamps (all adding up to the required postage amount) will add some major pizzazz to your mailing and allow it to stand out in mailboxes. And the best part of it all? This eye-catching (and profit-generating) trick won't cost your company, organization or school any more than the price of a regular, standard-looking stamp!

Alternatively, if you don't have the patience or time to paste four different stamps on each envelope, why not settle for one stamp... that has a unique shape? There are numerous stamps that deviate from the typical square, ho-hum look. Try a triangular shaped stamp that will be sure to stand out in a batch of envelopes. Or go for an oversized rectangle that guarantees to catch the recipient's eye – and arouse their curiosity.

As of late, the United States Postal Service authorized PC Postage – sets of personalized stamps that display your personal photo. There's no reason why businesses or organizations, shouldn't take advantage of this attention-grabbing opportunity. Just constructed a new building? Show it off on mailings for your donors to appreciate and admire. Launching a campaign for a new product? Why not put a photo of the product on the envelope's stamp? After all, how many people receive a mailing with stamps featuring products?

If you are doing an individualized, targeted mailing, be sure to send prospects a stamped envelope that reflects their interests.

For instance, one company I know of sold rare, miniature automobile collectibles. Seeking to boost sales, they obtained a mailing list (a topic in itself) and sent prospective clients mailings with a stamp on it that was sure to grab the attention of its recipient. Can you guess what was on the stamp? What else – an exotic car! Needless to say, the direct mail campaign was quite successful.

In all, stamps can be quite profitable for foreign countries, stamp collectors...and of course, businesses and non-profits as well.

BOTTOM LINE ACTION STEP:

Use creative stamps to stand out in the mailbox.

Rabbi Pinny Lipschutz is the publisher and editor of Yated Ne'eman, a respected Jewish newspaper. He once gave a marketing lecture for non-profit organizations where he captivated the audience with a speech on Rufus the Dog.

Rufus the *Who*?

Yeah, you read that correctly: Rufus the Dog.

"Okay," you're probably wondering. "What does a dog named Rufus have to do with marketing for non-profits?" Well, we were all wondering the same thing. Leave it up to the insightful Pinny Lipschutz to give us some pretty valuable advice, thanks to a five-year old bull terrier named Rufus.

Pinny paraphrased from an article in The New York Times (Hype, Money and Cornstarch: What It Takes to Win at Westminster – February 13, 2010). The article was about the annual Westminster Dog Show, which is a two-day extravaganza featuring thousands of dogs that are judged for beauty and pedigree; the winning dog is bestowed with a prize and becomes a sort of canine celebrity – albeit the type that barks their autograph.

But as the article so clearly pointed out, the choosing of a winning dog is often influenced by the serious advertising and marketing dollars spent on publicizing and hyping potential canine candidates in publications such as Dog News and Canine Chronicles. The ads are intended to create a unique brand image of the dog, generate major hype about its pedigree and hopefully influence the judges overseeing the competition.

Prices for advertising in these canine-based publications vary from $250 for a full-page black and white ad to a whopping $4,000 for the full-color cover (and you thought college tuition was expensive!).

But it's more than just ads that create hype. To build up an image as a show dog, canines and their handlers (the people who take care of the dog's needs and emotional well-being – and no, I'm not making this up!) must attend upwards of 150 dog shows each year to get the dog's name out in the open. Not to mention that the dogs possess their very own exclusive business cards for handlers to distribute out with the hopes of generating additional exposure.

While a top-notch campaign can easily cost more than $300,000 a year, the Westminster Dog Show's winner of 2006 – yes, our lovable "Rufus the Dog" – had a three-year marketing campaign that cost about $700,000, positively influencing his image nationwide and eventually leading him to be declared the winner.

Now back to Rabbi Lipschutz's timely topic: Getting the message out costs money – but as Rufus the Dog would agree, it's well worth the investment! So the obvious question remains: How do I spend my advertising dollars wisely?

While you may not be looking to compete at the Westminster Dog Show, you probably are looking for ways to generate exposure for your company and get your name out there. Print ads are an effective way to spread your corporate message. A major advantage of print advertising is the ability to choose which publications to best reach a business's potential customers.

For example, if you're seeking to grab the attention of the Asian marketplace, newspapers distributed in Asian communities are the perfect medium for doing so. On the other hand, if you're a dog food company seeking to attract the attention of every hungry mutt, the aforementioned Canine Chronicles is probably your best bet.

Of course, effective marketing also comes in the form of oversized posters, jumbo sized billboards and even those neon-yellow "50% Off Everything In Store!" sale signs displayed in a store's front window. In conjunction with print media, you can also utilize online media, radio commercials, direct mailings, trade shows and even bumper stickers to get your message out effectively.

So, take to heart the valuable lessons taught by Rufus the Dog and start barking the message out to your audience – you're almost guaranteed to become a winner!

BOTTOM LINE ACTION STEP:

Market with your eye on the prize.

MARKETING BASICS

> *The aim of marketing is to know and understand the customer so well, the product or service fits him and sells itself.*
>
> — Peter Drucker

THE RIGHT PLACE
& THE RIGHT TIME

The three keys to success for any effective marketing campaign are place, time and language. Let's take these thoughts one at a time.

In the world of marketing, place is placement. What is the best media for your message? For example, if you are aiming for a young audience, then it may be advisable to direct some of your marketing budget toward social networks. If you are looking to reach the business crowd, then one of your first choices would be the Wall Street Journal or Crain's, with its long-standing, loyal readership. If your campaign is targeting prospects via direct mail marketing, then you'll need to purchase a targeted list to reach qualified prospects.

Timing is everything, right? Did you ever notice that retail stores start advertising holiday sales before Thanksgiving? It makes perfect sense, because if your product is seasonal, you can't afford to wait until the season arrives to begin ramping up your efforts. If your organization is planning a fundraiser, you want people to save the date a couple of months in advance.

Last but not least, there is language, the message itself, which is the way in which you speak to your target audience. Whatever you do, I suggest that you make it as personal as possible. There is a West Coast based organization called "Mission Minded" which deals with the San Francisco Opera, the Levi Strauss Foundation and Stanford University to identify the most effective methods for attracting attention and getting results. They offered some great advice.

"Show the reader respect. Treat each one as an intelligent person. All communication is a transaction of time. Want a reader to think or act? Then offer a fair trade — by showing honest respect, delivering pertinent information, and making every word and image count.

"Respect is the rarest commodity in advertising driven by marketing interests that exploit our primitive anxieties. Authentic advertising in the public interest never treats the reader as a target to be manipulated, but as an aware and critical equal, constantly making perfectly understandable choices about where to spend his or her time."

BOTTOM LINE ACTION STEP:
Timing — and language — is everything.

The MARKETING RECIPE

Business trips can be exciting – and yes, even eye-opening experiences. Such was the business trip I once took to Chicago.

At my meeting with a highly regarded non-profit organization in Chicago, an executive board member challenged me with the following question: "You were here meeting with the faculty of all our divisions the entire day. You have a great picture of what we're all about, how we service the community and our vision for the future. Now tell me, what marketing plan would you implement to get our message out?"

I replied by explaining that although I spent the entire day taking notes about the organization's wonderful work, I would need a few days to analyze the data and develop a solid marketing plan. He proceeded to challenge me again. "I thought you're a marketing guru! You mean to tell me you can't tell me your plan of action now?!?"

I reiterated that every successful campaign needs careful planning and thought. At that point, another board member who has extensive experience in growing a business through marketing jumped in and defended my position – thank you Marc!

The reality is, a marketing campaign's level of success is directly linked to the planning and forethought put into it. The converse is also true. Countless marketing campaigns meet their demise for the opposing reason: a lack of proper planning.

As the legendary American statesman, scientist and philosopher, Benjamin Franklin, was often known to say, "By failing to prepare, you are preparing to fail." So let us now prepare to plan, and plan to succeed!

There's a special word in the marketing industry used to describe the process of outlining and designing a successful marketing plan: it's called a "Marketing Mix".

This term was coined in 1953 by Neil H. Borden, a prominent professor of marketing and advertising at the Harvard School of Business. Similar in concept to the recipe of your favorite food that details all the necessary ingredients, the "Marketing Mix" is a combination of different marketing components that come together to produce an effective marketing campaign.

Building on Borden's original "Marketing Mix" philosophy, Jerome McCarthy, a renowned marketer, established the **"Four P's"** concept in the early 1960's. According to McCarthy, the **"Four P's"** define the key tactical components of a "Marketing Mix" as: *Price; Placement; Product;* and *Promotion*. These components, when combined properly, serve as the catalyst for executing successful campaigns.

Sounds complicated? Think of the "Marketing Mix" as a tantalizing piece of strawberry shortcake. The cake contains flour, eggs, sugar, shortening and of course, strawberries. However, by altering the amounts and measurements of different ingredients, you can customize the cake according to your preferences.

For example, putting in more sugar will make the cake sweeter. If you're watching those calories, then less sugar will do – or simply use Splenda. For a rich, creamy frosting that will have you drooling, load up on the shortening and presto, you've made a strawberry shortcake aficionado's dream come true.

The same concept can be applied to the "Marketing Mix" and its **"Four P's."** The way you market your business or organization, can be altered simply by varying the Marketing Mix components.

Case in point: The Dollar Store increased its focus on the *pricing* component and placed less emphasis on the *product*, effectively positioning itself as a store for value-conscious consumers.

Alternatively, Swedish car manufacturer, Volvo, shied away from *pricing* and focused on the *product* component by stressing the *safety* benefits of their vehicles. It's no coincidence that Volvo is considered to be the car of choice for many physicians and professionals in the healthcare and wellness industry.

And car rental company, Avis, minimized both its *pricing* and *product* components, and successfully maximized its *placement* component by being the first car rental chain to have locations at all major airports. To date, Avis has over 4,000 branches worldwide. Ahh, the Marketing Mix at work.

SECTION V MARKETING BASICS

As illustrated from the above examples, these companies strategically tweaked the components contained within their "Marketing Mix" and used it to their advantage – but only by sitting down and putting some serious thought into their "Marketing Mix". And there's no reason why your business or organization shouldn't be doing the same as well.

BOTTOM LINE ACTION STEP:

There are many practical and lucrative benefits that the Marketing Mix and its Four P's has to offer. Harness the power of these marketing strategies to grow your business and boost profits.

117

SOME BLUE LABEL PLEASE!

Once upon a time, back when a pack of bubble gum cost only a nickel, a person wanting to buy a new car walked into their local car dealership and looked around.

If he didn't have a lot of money, he would choose a simple car called Chevrolet. If he was able to splurge a bit more on leather seats and a radio, a Buick was the vehicle of choice. And if he was really looking to impress the neighbors with a vehicle boasting every possible amenity, a luxurious Cadillac was the way to go.

All these vehicles were manufactured by a large American company known as General Motors. Their vehicles were clearly labeled and defined according to a consumer's level of income and social status; choosing a car was, in essence, a simple process.

Now fast-forward half a century.

Want a car to impress the neighbors with? Try a Chevrolet Corvette for $62,000. Looking for a low-cost vehicle? Why not try the Chevrolet

Malibu at only $17,000. Looking for an expensive car? Try the Cadillac Escalade for only $60,000. Still can't decide on a cheap car? Cadillac, the upscale carmaker, offers vehicles for as low as $28,000.

Confused? That's okay... According to many economists and prominent marketers, a lack of proper focus on their product elements was the reason why GM had economic difficulties in 2009.

Which leads us to back to our topic of: **"The Four P's"**.

"The Four P's" represent the key tactical components of a Marketing Mix – **Product, Price, Placement** and **Promotion**. Let's focus on: Product.

While there are many elements that make up the Product category, let's focus on one of the hottest buzzwords in today's marketplace – product positioning. Positioning is, in essence, the way consumers identify and view your product. It involves forming a specific image of your company, organization or service in the mind of a consumer.

Want to fully understand what the power of positioning does?

Imagine your best friend was just made a partner in a law firm and you want to buy him a nice present. You know he enjoys (and may now need!) a good drink every now and then, so you decide to buy him something that he can drink to celebrate after successfully closing a deal or after a long hard day. Here are two very different scenarios:

SCENARIO A:

> You present your friend with a magnificently shaped glass bottle. A liter of amber-colored liquid sits in the bottle. And there, sitting proudly on the bottle's front are the words: "Johnnie Walker Blue Label." The appreciative smile on his face tells you that your thoughtful gift has hit the spot.

SCENARIO B:

> You present your friend with a simple shaped glass bottle. A liter of amber-colored liquid sits in the bottle. And there, sitting not-so-proudly on the bottle's front are the words: "Joe's Imitation Style Whiskey." (There goes your good friend!)

The fact is, thanks to Johnnie Walker's clever positioning, consumers automatically perceive a bottle of Blue Label as a high-quality, great-tasting product – even without trying it (although it IS good!). On the flip side, a bottle of whiskey with a cheap, no-name brand on its label will not make for a very memorable gift.

Now let's take this concept a step further. Once you have success-fully positioned your company, you have now created a product brand, also known as branding. The term branding originates from the days when cowboys would actually stamp words onto their cattle to help identify flocks grazing on the open prairie. In a similar vein, by branding your product, you have psychologically stamped your identity into the minds of consumers, effectively creating an exclu-sive brand image for your product.

Product positioning and branding is essential for the success of a product – be it a business, organization or service. Time and time again, it has been proven that those with a unique positioning angle are able to reap higher dividends from their marketing campaigns and generate superior results.

BOTTOM LINE ACTION STEP:

Make sure your product is conveying the right image and is branded for success.

WATCH
your POSITION...

In the world of advertising and marketing, the concept of differentiating a business or product from its competition is known as Positioning. Positioning is a way of portraying something in a unique, distinct way – and forming a specific image of your business, organization, or product in the mind of a consumer.

For a simple lesson on Positioning, just look at any highly paid executive on Wall Street – a prime example of dressing for the pinnacle of success. Picture the expensive Italian suit, the luxurious silk tie, the designer leather shoes, and the stylish gold watch.

That watch is actually a marketing lesson in itself.

Chances are, the watch wasn't purchased in a discount store. It would be safe to assume that the watch probably boasts a face emblazoned with the name of an upscale watch company, such as Rolex, Cartier or Movado.

Wondering why the Rolex ended up positioned on the wrists of successful executives and not a Casio watch? Blame it on "branding and positioning!"

For a deeper understanding, let's examine the Rolex positioning angle to understand the many cogs and wheels churning behind this powerful concept called "positioning."

Rolex portrays itself as the king of the timepiece industry, the royalty of watches. That exclusivity manifests itself in the quality of their watches, extravagant ads, lavish packaging... and of course, the legendary Rolex price tag.

One would be foolish to argue that an achievement such as making VP at an investment bank or partner at a prestigious law firm wouldn't qualify deserving of a luxurious Rolex watch. Quite the contrary, the fancy title and the well deserved promotion demands a posh Rolex timepiece to lend its regal bearings to the magnificence of the event. In essence, Rolex positioned itself in the mind of consumers as the upscale watch worthy of being worn at momentous occasions.

Such is the power of positioning.

Now contrast Rolex with Casio – yes, the Casio brand that makes those black plastic watches retailing for $5.99 in the rollback section at Walmart. Let us assume that Casio began retailing gold watches costing $2,000 a piece. Would one even dream of purchasing it with their bonus (...even with the gold!) Of course not! The positioning of Casio's watches effectively sentence its fate to the cold metal shelving racks at your local pharmacy.

But that's not necessarily a bad thing.

After all, who would send their energetic teenagers to summer camp with an expensive Movado timepiece? Along with the socks, undershirts, pajamas (and tons of junk food!), responsible parents pack a – what else? – Casio watch! And so, while a Casio watch is not intended for every occasion, neither is a Movado timepiece. In essence, that is what positioning is all about.

Time and time again, I see that companies, organizations and politicians with a unique positioning angle are able to reap higher dividends from their marketing campaigns and generate extremely successful results.

BOTTOM LINE ACTION STEP:

Figure out where your product is best positioned and create a marketing plan to get it there.

REVISITING *the* CLASSIC AVIS CAMPAIGN

Ahh, summer. Thoughts of summer conjure up images of rejuvenating sunshine, colorful flowers – and pesky mosquitoes.

While we all have had our fair share of mosquito encounters in our own backyards, that pales in comparison to the mosquito horrors that plague hikers camping outdoors for weeks at a time. And that is precisely how we lead into another one of our P's - <u>product positioning</u> (remember the Four P's – Product, Price, Placement and Promotion?).

Traditionally, tent manufacturers marketed their products to hikers and outdoor aficionados with a positioning angle boasting the spaciousness of tents or amenities that came with it. However, good ol' innovation came along and changed the way outdoor tents were marketed.

You see, hikers wanted more than just big tents with built-in cup holders. They also wanted to be rid of those itchy, annoying mosquito bites that were inevitably linked to their outdoor expeditions ("Hey Seth, your red, bumpy arms didn't seem to enjoy the trip, huh?!").

Thanks to a little creativity and lots of pesticide, a new invention was born: ITNs, short for Insecticide Treated Nets. Basically, it was a net that hung over the opening of a tent. The net was treated with a powerful chemical that would kill mosquitoes on contact, ensuring that hikers (and their arms) remained bite free.

And so, the outdated sales message of spaciousness and amenities was slowly pushed aside as savvy tent companies began positioning their outdoor gear as mosquito repellent – and taking a huge bite out of the competition in the process (pun intended). Indeed, a classic example of product positioning and its tremendous power.

Now here's the obvious question that you're probably asking: "How can I apply these positioning concepts to my business?" Here goes!

- *Firstly, don't be afraid to distinguish your company, organization or product in a different light. While you don't want to appear too outrageous or extreme, standing out from the rest of the pack is a good thing.*

One of the classic examples taught in marketing was the campaign created by advertising legend Bill Bernbach of DDB for the car rental giant, Avis. Instead of portraying Avis as yet another car rental agency that "is the best and the biggest, offers quality, blah-blah-blah," Avis captured the public's attention – and wallets – through the following positioning angle and slogan: "We try harder." Avis ranked as the number two car rental agency at that time, behind the industry's number one company, Hertz. The positioning angle was that at #2, we will try harder to please our customers.

While most companies won't want to admit they're number two, Avis did more than just admit it – they used it to their marketing advantage. And believe it or not, this distinct way of positioning their brand and product was a great success. Within a year of launching the campaign Avis had tripled its market share to 35%.

By positioning themselves as the underdogs (against Hertz who were the industry leaders), Avis attracted clients based on their promise to give them that extra bit of service and care – because after all, they were only number two in the rental industry and couldn't afford to lose any customers.

- *Secondly, while it is generally advisable to portray your product in an appealing and positive light, at times, a "shock effect" can be employed to successfully market to your consumers.*

Such as the method devised by mouthwash company, Listerine. In their quest to outsell Scope, the marketing whizzes at Listerine realized that repeating the same old "tastes great, freshens breath" mouthwash mantra just wasn't going to work. So they settled for the "shock effect."

Their positioning angle? "Listerine: The taste you hate twice a day."

While you can be sure that some jaws dropped (and dentures slipped) in the boardroom when this positioning angle was introduced, it is undoubtedly brilliant.

By portraying their product in this light (via the "shock effect"), Listerine is basically telling consumers: "Yeah, our product may not taste that great...but have some pity for the guy you're talking too!" To really get rid of those bacteria particles and nasty germs sitting in your mouth, throw out those bottles of sweet, gentle-tasting mouthwash and settle for some powerful, germ-killing Listerine!

The bottom line? Put serious thought into what your product is and what it does. Get a little creative with portraying your brand's image. And don't be scared to be a little different. Because whether it's the mouthwash you hate, the mosquitoes you detest, or the rental car company you love, it's the power of marketing that can make all the difference between failure...and success.

BOTTOM LINE ACTION STEP:

Think out of the box when positioning your product. With a little creativity, your product's brand will be positioned solidly above the rest.

DRINK...& DRIVE *your* BUSINESS

Super Bowl Sunday usually guarantees several things – among them: groups sitting around a large television set, consuming large quantities of unhealthy, albeit very tasty food, and ice cold beer. After all, what would a Super Bowl Sunday be without a host handing out ice-cold bottles of Budweiser to his guests?

Alternatively, if you are a marketer attending a Super Bowl party, you could also ponder another question, compliments of the Four P's: where would those numerous bottles of beer be without the marketing power of Product Positioning?

For those in the know, it's not just a good question – it's an expensive one.

According to the Marin Institute (a supervising industry group), the alcohol industry spends over $5 billion a year on advertising and marketing. And for good reason. Because you see, alcoholic beverage products are mostly about image and positioning.

For example, Budweiser portrays itself as the everyday, domestic beer. Michelob, on the other hand, gives off the impression of imported exclusivity, right down to the label proudly proclaiming "Premium Beer." But here's the kicker – both beer companies are owned and produced by the same manufacturer, Anheuser-Busch. Surprised? You shouldn't be. Because truthfully speaking, most beer companies make similar malt products – it's simply the positioning that differentiates them.

Claude Hopkins, the legendary advertising genius (referred to by many as The Father of Modern Advertising), understood this concept quite well when he was hired in 1920 to produce a campaign for the Schlitz Beer Company.

At that point in time, the marketing message being promoted by beer companies was that their beers were "Pure." In fact, companies were taking out double-page print ads in magazines just to write the word "Pure" in oversized letters. However, companies didn't bother delving into the specifics and explaining to consumers what exactly made their beer pure – until Claude Hopkins came along.

While taking a tour of the beer factory to see how Schlitz Beer could create a unique positioning niche, Hopkins stumbled across a large room where thousands of empty glass bottles were being sprayed with hot steam. Upon asking what purpose this served, Hopkins was told that the bottles were being sterilized with boiling steam before being filled with beer.

(Note: In 1920, plastic had not yet been invented and manufacturing new glass bottles was a costly process. Beer companies would clean and reuse the glass bottles returned by their customers, refill them with beer and repackage them for sale.)

Hopkins was incredulous when he saw the bottle-steaming process. "So why don't you tell your customers about this complicated steaming and sterilization process that's done to the bottles they buy?" he asked the owners of Schlitz. "But it's hardly anything special," came the reply. "Every beer company does this to their bottles."

"That may be," Hopkins countered. "However, other companies have never told customers about this intricate sterilization process – you will!" And so, Claude Hopkins created a memorable campaign focusing on what actually made Schlitz Beer so pure, capping it with the tag line: Schlitz Beer – Washed with live steam.

Within a few months, Schlitz was outselling the competition, soaring from fifth place to first in the alcoholic beverage marketplace – thanks to insightful marketing.

Now let's think about what Hopkins did and how his unique insights can be applied to your everyday marketing practices.

Did Hopkins come up with a brilliant, earth-shattering brainstorm? Hardly! Rather, he simply educated prospective customers about how things were done in the Schlitz beer-making process – not coincidentally, the very same process used by competitors. But, by being first to lay claim, he created a truly unique positioning niche and image in the minds of consumers.

Likewise, whether you own a company, have an organization or sell a product, it is important to put some thought into the cogs and wheels behind them – and inform clients of these seemingly minor things. While something about your particular entity may seem trivial to you (just like the sterilization process appeared inconsequential to the makers of Schlitz Beer), that very same thing may prove to be a tremendous selling point for prospective clients.

So, whether you're selling bottles of beer or just lifting one up during the half-time show, raise that bottle high and be sure to toast the many lucrative benefits of proper Product Positioning!

BOTTOM LINE ACTION STEP:

Position your product in a way that differentiates itself from others, and communicate this difference to your customers.

POSITIONING & PACKAGING H$_2$O

Ahhh ... the lazy days of summer. The air conditioners humming and the bright sun illuminating the world. Summertime at its best!

The summer season always ushers in a marketing potpourri of products including sunscreen, swimming accessories, and of course, drinks to keep you hydrated.

Walk into any supermarket, stroll past the oversized display of portable barbecue grills and folding lawn chairs, then head toward the beverage aisle and take a look around. The selection available is absolutely overwhelming.

You can choose from a plethora of drinks such as water, juice, soda, fruit-flavored drinks and even powerful energy drinks loaded with vitamins to propel the space shuttle into orbit. How is it possible for the manufacturers of these drinks to compete in such a cluttered arena? Well, for some companies, it's easier than others. Especially for the beverage company whose cleverly designed labels, thought-provoking flavor names and refined color schemes have launched it into super-stardom.

Hello, VitaminWater!

As per an insightful article that a friend sent me from a blog called Point2Agent, the wildly successful VitaminWater drink – which popularized the idea of "enhanced water" and which was acquired by Coca-Cola in 2007 for $4.1 billion – revolutionized the way people viewed beverages.

Founded in 1996 by J. Darius Bikoff after conceiving the idea of blending pure mineral water, anti-oxidants and vitamins in a tasty yet healthy blend, the company captured the public's attention by creating a very unique and distinct niche for itself. Their marketing mix clearly demonstrates how by properly understanding markets and creating different sales approaches, one can truly take their company to the top. Here are a few marketing ideas that we can all learn from VitaminWater:

CREATE YOUR OWN MARKET –

> Sure, there were drinks similar to VitaminWater before the brand even existed, but they were all lumped together in the homogeneous beverage category. VitaminWater merely took the existing segment and began marketing it under a new name and concept – enhanced water. It wasn't necessarily the product itself that was a success; rather the positioning behind it.

DON'T (NECESSARILY) FOLLOW THE TREND –

> Go to any store that sells beverages and you will be greeted with an eyeful of outrageous logos, zany advertising, and similar packaging and messaging...and then you will see Vitamin-Water. The minimalist packaging and stark design is quite a departure from the norm, but to the consumer it is much more memorable and a reflection of the brand's individuality.

DETAILS COUNT TOO –

Even if the product itself isn't what you expected, the small details like the bottle notes can lead to gratifying and memorable experience. Every flavor comes replete with its own "mini-biography" on the side that both entertains and informs the drinker...and keeps the product in one's mind long after the bottle is finished.

MARKET WITH INTELLIGENCE –

Hitting the right people in the right places can be the "make-or-break" for a brand. VitaminWater's target market is adults who are relatively health-conscious and give thought to what they drink each day. And their clean packaging, crisp bottle notes and distinctive advertising cater precisely to that particular demographic.

BOTTOM LINE ACTION STEP:

Do proper research, understand your target market, position from a unique angle, then develop creative packaging.

GETTING THE MESSAGE OUT – ANATOMY _of_ A CAMPAIGN

Over the years, my firm, Bottom Line Marketing Group, has presented several unique fundraising and marketing seminars geared towards executive directors, development professionals and lay leaders representing non-profit organizations from around the world. These seminars take months of planning, research and – what else? – marketing to attract participants.

I've been asked many times to detail a sample campaign. Naturally, the specific tactics of any client's marketing are confidential; however, for my own campaign, I can get away with it! Therefore, here is a detailed anatomy of the marketing campaign we undertook to promote the conferences.

PRINT ADVERTISEMENTS —
While online banners and e-mail marketing are definitely the rage in today's high-tech world, good old print ads have yet to go out of style. The benefits offered by full-scale newspaper print ads are numerous.

First, they're simple to read! Many web advertisements involve scrolling with a computer mouse to view the complete image or clicking on different links to see the entire ad – all of which can ultimately lead to viewer disinterest. With a newspaper advertisement, it's all there in the reader's hands instantaneously. And to get the biggest bang for your advertising dollar, be sure to post the ad in high-profile places – such as a banner ad on the front cover of a prominent newspaper.

Second, print ads guarantee that your advertising will be seen the way you design it – true WYSIWYG (what you see is what you get).

PRESS RELEASES —

While a traditional print ad can work wonders, couple it together with a timely press release and the results will absolutely amaze you! Aside from the fact that most newspapers generally don't charge to post press releases (making the cost of it completely free!), an article about your business in the paper adds credibility to your image. After all, if a company is written up in a national newspaper, there's probably something big and important about it! In addition, press release can be featured in many newspapers, magazines and websites targeting a specific demographic.

E-MAIL —

There's nothing like a personalized message waiting for you inside your e-mail account's inbox! Chances are, you probably have numerous e-mail addresses of business associates, clients, friends and relatives. These people are all considered potential target markets for upcoming events or offers that you may be launching. So be sure to get the word out with an e-mail blast to those privileged to be in your address book – and ask them to forward the message to their friends and associates as well.

The best thing about e-mail advertising is that it's quite cost-effective and time-efficient. The quickest way of getting your message out via e-mail – and to avoid getting blacklisted as spam – is to harness the power of an e-mail service provider such as *iContact* or *Constant Contact,* in tandem with your contact list which should be developed and expanded over time.

DIRECT MAIL —

When it comes to targeted marketing, direct mail is the king! For starters, you don't have to worry about a direct mail piece accidently directed directly into somebody's spam box, being skipped over by a newspaper reader or not getting published in a newspaper column. Fact is, if it ends up in a person's mailbox, it'll get seen. Of course, the attention it receives depends on the interest of the recipient (a lengthy topic in itself).

Furthermore, unlike most other methods, direct mailers allow for the inclusion of a return card/envelope that enables the recipient to conveniently respond to your direct mail solicitation. And direct mail offers you an opportunity for keeping track of who responds and, most importantly, creates what's known as a *Housefile* – the marketing term used to describe a valuable list of prime prospects for future mailing campaigns.

WEBSITE AND ONLINE BANNER ADS —

A special website was created for the conference as well as banner ads that directly linked it to the website.

WORD OF MOUTH —

Have others help get your message out. Whether it's through verbal referrals or online posts, the recommendation of others can prove quite valuable. In fact, one of our previous seminar attendees – a well respected and highly regarded personality – was so impressed with the seminar, that he posted a glowing message about it on a web page used exclusively and viewed by many others within his industry throughout the world, creating much buzz in the process. It also must be pointed out that to rely on marketing via word of mouth, the other forms of multi-channel marketing must be employed in order for a) people to talk about your event, product, etc. and b) to have some ability to control the message. The other forms of marketing gives "viral marketing" the necessary talking points.

RADIO —

Additionally, having a prominent radio host discussing your event can really have people buzzing. In our case, we were fortunate to secure interviews with noted radio personality, Nachum Segal.

So, when you're ready to grow your business, contact a reputable marketing agency familiar with all the different methods of multi-channel marketing – from newspaper ads to billboards outside the Lincoln Tunnel in New York City, and everything in between – to help you get your message out effectively, swiftly and successfully.

BOTTOM LINE ACTION STEP:

Use a variety of mediums to get your message out with a well thought out, well planned, well executed marketing campaign.

LET'S TALK ABOUT WORD *of* MOUTH ADVERTISING!

The prime objective of a marketing campaign is to get the word out to your target market. Many try to accomplish this by using a form of speech to get the message across – something known in the marketing industry as "word of mouth advertising." However, it's not as simple as it may seem.

During a strategy session before a marketing campaign's launch, you sit in a boardroom sporting a suit and tie, relating the ideas necessary to launch an effective promotion. While the primary message of any campaign is to get people talking about your service or product, the guidance provided by things such as advertisements and newsletters ensures that your corporate message doesn't get muddled by uninformed people talking about your company.

Often, people ask me: "Why bother with advertising or marketing expenses? Let me just focus on word of mouth techniques by having people tell their friends about my product! After all, what's more trustworthy than hearing about a product from a person you know and whose opinion you value?"

Without getting overly technical, here's the deal.

139

Word of mouth techniques are very valuable and can certainly help a business generate buzz. However, there must be something driving the word of mouth and steering it in the right direction to guarantee that the buzz doesn't stray off your targeted messaging and create havoc.

New York Times bestselling author John Maxwell discusses this in his groundbreaking book, "The 17 Indisputable Laws of Teamwork." In the chapter, "The Law of Communication," Mr. Maxwell highlights how, when people don't communicate effectively, the results can be quite comical – and confusing.

Imagine this (all-too-familiar) scenario:

Mother says to her younger daughter Rebecca:
> Your grandparents are coming for dinner tonight. Can you tell your sister Sarah to put on her shoes, run to the corner store and buy a box of that blueberry herbal tea that your grandmother enjoys so much?

Rebecca says to her father:
> Grandma and Grandpa are coming to dinner tonight. Mommy said Sarah needs to get a box of blueberry herbal tea, so she should put on her shoes and go.

Father says to Sarah:
> Mommy said you should put on your Burberry shoes and go because grandma and grandpa are coming to dinner tonight.

Sarah to Mommy:
> I never bought those Burberry shoes because they didn't fit, remember? And why can't I stay and have dinner with grandma and grandpa. Are they mad at me?

A very confused Mommy.
> Huh? I never mentioned anything about Burberry shoes. What in the world are you talking about?! Of course you are staying for dinner. And where is the tea you were supposed to pick up. Your grandparents are going to be here any minute.

While you may find this dysfunctional, broken-telephone scenario hilarious, it really isn't quite funny when the message of your business gets distorted as it's passed from consumer to consumer. So what is the solution to ensure that it remains precise and "stays on message?" By having a marketing campaign that runs concurrently, guiding consumers and keeping their conversations about your entity going in the right direction.

As you stroll along the street in any given city, or through the mall in any suburb, take a good look at the strollers used for pushing along the little ones – chances are, you'll see some smiling tykes cruising around in a fashionable stroller known as a Bugaboo. The obvious question begs to be asked: How did this upstart Dutch company experience such a surge in popularity, overshadowing established companies that have been in the business for decades?

Chalk one up for "word of mouth advertising" – and the strategic marketing campaign behind it. Bugaboo capitalized on word of mouth techniques by having famous celebrities wheel their babies around in Bugaboos, generating tremendous word of mouth publicity.

But that alone wasn't enough.

Bugaboo simultaneously launched a bold advertising campaign highlighting the stroller's originality and innovative design, giving consumers a tangible reason to consider the stroller instead of just shrugging it off as a passing fad. It was the use of both important elements that propelled Bugaboo into stroller stardom.

So at the day's end, the lesson should be as clear and undistorted as possible: when word of mouth advertising goes together with an effective marketing campaign it ensures focused communication, and targeted messaging.

BOTTOM LINE ACTION PLAN:

Start a word of mouth campaign by first having a solid planned marketing campaign in place to keep the word of mouth campaign on the right course.

The ELEVATOR PITCH...

Picture this: You're visiting the office building of a potential client and stand waiting for the elevator while silently rehearsing your sales presentation.

As the chime dings and elevator doors whisk open, the CEO of the company you've come to solicit business from suddenly walks in and situates himself right next to you. The doors close and it's just you and him standing there for the next 22 seconds as the elevator quickly ascends to the forty-something floor.

For the next 22 seconds, you will have his complete and undivided attention. There will be no ringing phones, interruptions by secretaries or distracting employees that can potentially hamper your attempts at landing this account. But one problem still remains: how are you supposed to deliver a successful sales pitch in less than 30 seconds?

Welcome to the world of marketing.

In this industry, 30 second sales pitches are quite the norm. Of course, the sales pitch may come in the form of a newspaper print advertisement rather than a face-to-face meeting, but the premise is just the same.

Studies show that the average reader spends only a few seconds looking at an advertisement before turning the page. Those few seconds are crucial to capturing the reader's interest and entice them to continue reading your advertisement.

Hence, the "Elevator Pitch" – a term referring to delivering a sales pitch within the short time frame of a typical elevator ride. This concept is used to assure that an ad is succinct enough to give over a basic message to the reader accurately and quickly without losing their attention.

Often, an advertisement will be cluttered with headlines, sub-headlines and lots of text in an attempt to provide the reader with every bit of information about a company or product. But as the old adage goes, less is more.

A good ad often starts with an idea that can be relayed via a visual image or clever sentence – and sometimes through both. The visual can be a photo of the actual product, a person interacting with the product or an end result that occurs because of the product. The sentence can be a provocative headline, a humorous pun or general message relating to the product or service being advertised.

Recently, my firm, Bottom Line Marketing Group created a new campaign that has generated fantastic feedback and an impressive response. So why not use that as an example of how to create a winning ad?

The layout of this ad was user-friendly and straightforward. The advertisement displayed a photo evoking the image of a summer getaway. A catchy headline on top grabbed the reader's interest by highlighting the problem that many businesses face in the summertime and offered a practical solution.

When the reader had been adequately informed about the offer, their eyes then shifted to the prominently displayed phone number on the bottom that directed them to call and find out more. The fax and e-mail address were also listed, allowing viewers to use the contact method of their choice.

Best of all, readers were persuaded to learn more about how that service can help their business by featuring authentic testimonials from satisfied business owners who have benefited from that company.

Lastly, the advertisement was produced in full-color, which according to numerous studies, has a 40% higher readership score than standard black and white advertisements.

So, before the elevator doors open, keep in mind that although there are many secrets to guarantee successful results from your advertising campaign, primary among them is communicating your message in a brief way.

BOTTOM LINE ACTION STEP:

1. Advertise!

2. Keep message concise.

3. Save the details for your company's brochure and website.

6 TIPS
for CREATING
EFFECTIVE WEBSITES

Once upon a time, people looking to market their product or service went to an agency and launched a campaign.

The campaign would consist of placing ads in targeted newspapers and magazines, an ad in the Yellow Pages, and perhaps a direct mail campaign and billboard. And if they were particularly aggressive – and depending on the nature of the business – they would do some creative marketing like blowing up a dozen helium balloons with their logo emblazoned on the side and hand it out to young children walking down the block.

Well, up until 20 years ago, that pretty much was the scope of most marketing campaigns. However, today with the way the internet is integrated into every business, those methods need to be supplemented along with newer forms of marketing for today's world.

First and foremost, every reputable company competing in today's business arena must possess a website to maintain an online presence. Of course, that entails creating a site that will attract, inform and most importantly, impress potential clients, while engaging current clients. Some companies actually can benefit from an e-commerce website (making purchases of products online). However this article focuses on "corporate websites" – sites that inform and educate prospects about your company.

Below are the 6 tips for creating an effective website for your company:

1. **KEEP IT NICE!**

   A website must adhere to certain design basics such as easy navigation, correct page weights and browser capability, to name just a few. Be sure to discuss these details with a reputable web development firm and analyze what's best for your particular site's needs.

   When Bottom Line Marketing Group developed our revolutionary platform – known as WebsiteWithBrains.com – the development team spent quite a bit of time tinkering with these fine details to guarantee a pleasant browsing experience. Because we all know that looks matter...especially when it's *your* website.

2. **KEEP IT FRESH!**

   Your customers won't touch a bottle of milk with an old expiration date – so why do you think that they'll spend time on your web page if everything is outdated and archaic? It's crucial that you continuously update the website with timely information, current news and up-to-date sales and/or discounts taking place.

3. **KEEP IT CLEAR!**
   Make certain that your contact information is clearly visible and accessible on your website. After all, the point of a site isn't to impress people with its amazing graphics and user interface – rather, it's to bring you more business! Be sure to have phone numbers and addresses (both postal and e-mail) displayed prominently on your site. Remember: They can't contact you unless they know how to reach you!

4. **KEEP IT PIXEL-PERFECT!**
   Websites are so valuable precisely because they allow for more than just paragraphs of text to describe your service or product. Viewers can be enticed by pixel-perfect photos of your operation, a hi-resolution image that piques their interest or even a brief video clip that highlights the importance of what you have to offer.

   Lastly, while stock photos can be used, try wherever possible to use photos of real people. Real photos will generate a better response compared to generic photos.

5. **KEEP IT TRUE!**
   The best way to make a sale? Have somebody else do it for you! There's nothing more powerful than an authentic, well-written testimonial from a satisfied client. Every website should have a page displaying testimonials from real people.

   However, do be careful: your prospective clients are not naïve. Simply writing a paragraph about how great your company is and vaguely signing it with the initials "L.D.C. – Newark, NJ" won't do much in terms of generating credibility (the same goes for signing off as "Anonymous").

6. **KEEP IT SIMPLE!**

There's nothing more irritating then navigating through a website that appears to have been created exclusi vely for rocket scientists and brain surgeons. Your potential customer's don't want to invest time or energy trying to figure out how to get basic information from the website. Ensure that search functionality is simple and that all the options are clearly displayed on the home page.

In a nutshell, when creating your website, keep all these points in mind for a powerful site that will effectively communicate what your company does.

BOTTOM LINE ACTION STEP:

A website is a crucial marketing vehicle for any company today.

LONG LIVE *the* KING ... PAPER!

If you want people to get their hands on your product, you've got to put something in their hands first. It could be a catalog, postcard, glossy brochure or a newspaper or magazine advertisement. When you give the customer an experience he can feel, he is more likely to be your next buyer.

Recently after I arrived home from work, I opened my mailbox and an oversized postcard jumped out (from amongst the bills...!) It helped, of course, that the postcard was from a company whose successful marketing techniques I really admire: Bed, Bath & Beyond. When the last recession hit, this company didn't clamp down on their marketing – actually, they ramped it up – especially their 20% coupon special. It's no wonder that soon after, the company announced record earnings and their stock hit an all-time high.

While the conventional wisdom over the past decade was declaring that "print is dead," Bed Bath & Beyond knows that people of all ages respond to direct mail. The folks at Retail Online Integration, who advocate the diversified use of several advertising and marketing venues, say you get a longer attention span with print, a longer shelf life, and a higher perceived value. The pressing issues for the future, they say, are determining how your print catalogs work in a cross-channel environment, and the right mix of print and electronic media for your brand.

A short while ago, five of the nation's leading magazine publishers embarked on a multimillion-dollar advertising campaign promoting the "power of print" in this online, digital era in which we live. Some of the statistics they issued were eye-opening. Four out of five Americans read magazines and spend an average of 43 minutes reading them. Who says we don't have long attention spans anymore?

Sure some companies are putting their catalogs on line in page-flipping digital formats. You click your mouse on the pages or show off your dexterity in finger-swiping to turn the pages. This is certainly a marketing phenomenon worth watching, and would seem at the moment, a great way of leveraging the print version. But nevertheless, print based marketing cannot be thrown away.

You may have seen the holiday mailer Bottom Line produced for Le Chocolatier Extraordinaire. It may have even shown up in your mailbox one night, and I am certain you found it too big of a treat to discard.

My good friend, Yonah Blumenfrucht came to us with a challenge. They wanted us to help them generate new leads for their core business of gift baskets during the increasingly competitive holiday season. To help them do this, and to set them apart from competitors, our creative team produced a beautiful, cost-effective "mini" catalog that showcased their delectable chocolates and stunning gift baskets.

There is an art and science to creating effective retail and business to business catalogs. Catalogs need beautiful photography to effectively showcase products, hard-hitting and concise copywriting to make the sales pitch, a strong call to action throughout the piece, accurate mailing lists to reach the right audience and a keen understanding of how best to organize and position content for maximum ROI (Return On Investment). We arranged all of this for them, and the results were really sweet.

We're not debating whether electronic media works. It does and we use it too for suitable clients and target markets, but print is still king and will always play a critical role in any marketing mix.

BOTTOM LINE ACTION STEP:

On your next marketing campaign don't squint when someone says use print. Instead, sprint!

STICKING WITH *the* PROGRAM

You just started an advertising campaign with great expectations, not to mention with a sizable investment. Much to your dismay, the days pass and your campaign does not seem to be having the result that you dreamed of. Do you give it more time, or do you cut and run?

How long do you stick with an advertising campaign that seems to be floundering? This is an important and fair question, which can only be answered after taking a combination of factors into account.

The three most important aspects to consider are:

1. Is your message "resonating," which means can people relate to it?
2. Are you targeting the right audience with the right medium?
3. Did you allocate enough resources to the campaign?

Unless you are advertising a spectacular closeout sale, the rule of thumb is it could take a good 3 to 6 months, of real market penetration, to see results from your campaign. Even with that passage of time, a decision to pull the plug should never be taken in a vacuum or be based solely on emotion. You probably worked hard to map the campaign so it is equally worthwhile to figure out if it is really off track.

Recently, a client called and said, "I know you counseled patience, but the response is weak and I'm concerned." I recommended that we assemble a small focus group to obtain impartial feedback. The client came by with three people that he selected and we asked them some very specific questions. From their answers, we could see that each was giving messages back based on the creative approach that we took. This means the message was resonating, so I advised my client that it would be premature to cut it short.

Barring positive proof that your message is not clicking, the only other valid reasons for halting a campaign early is if you are getting feedback that is inconsistent with your messaging, or if it is obvious that you have chosen the wrong medium to reach your target audience.

There can be other reasons why an ad campaign fails that have nothing to do with the medium or the message. You must always level with yourself, and your marketing firm, about any flaws or weaknesses to your product or service. I cannot overemphasize the importance of this. Just as you must confide all of your symptoms to your doctor, and just as you have to tell your lawyer the whole truth and nothing but the truth, a prospective client has to come clean with his marketing firm.

Of course, a qualified marketing firm can help you put the right spin on your product and service. A professional expert understands how to communicate with an audience effectively. But sometimes, the product lacks sizzle.

One of the classic text book examples of a failed advertising campaign began in April, 1985. After 100 years of making good, old-fashioned Coca-Cola, the company brought New Coke to the market, with a new formula designed to compete with Pepsi. Coca-Cola launched a splashy advertising campaign, hiring a famous comedian to promote it. When sales fizzled, Coke initially thought they picked the wrong guy to plug it. Less than two months later, when market research showed people would rather drink the classic formula, they pulled the plug on New Coke and poured it down the drain.

There is a second lesson to be learned from the Coca-Cola experience. If a company that has been around 100 years must advertise to keep its name before the public, then all the more so, a lesser-known organization must advertise too.

The worst mistake, other than pulling a plug prematurely, is never to plug yourself at all because you think it is too expensive.

A few years ago, Dr. Bill Siegel, Chairman & CEO of Longwoods International, a respected leader in brands strategy, conducted research into Colorado's flagging tourism industry. In 1993, Colorado became the only state to eliminate its tourism marketing function, and cut its $12 million promotion budget to zero. By 1995, Colorado's domestic market share plunged 30% and in the important summer resort segment, Colorado plummeted from 1st to 17th place among the 50 states.

To make a long story short, it took 14 long years and a new, higher $19 million budget for Colorado to rebound to an all-time tourism high. Fourteen years is a long time to wait to overcome a strategic mistake. It's a lot easier to give an advertising campaign a few more weeks, or even months, to see if it will gain traction.

"The Colorado saga provides a cautionary tale for financial decision-makers who, in these difficult economic times, are naturally looking at major cutbacks in all areas, including promotion," wrote Dr. Siegel. "It clearly illustrates that marketing is an essential net generator of revenue and profits to the organization, not a cost."

BOTTOM LINE ACTION STEP:

Don't cut and run until you've sat and thought!

SECTION VI:
MARKETING INITIATIVES

" Many a small thing has been made large by the right kind of advertising. "

— Mark Twain

MOLTEN LAVA MARKETING

It's not easy living in Iceland. No, I'm not saying this because of the perpetual cold and icy weather that the country is famous for.

Do you remember the eruption in 2010 of Iceland's Eyjafjallajökull volcano, which crippled all European air travel for nearly a full month?

The Washington Post detailed the severe consequences resulting from ash spread by the volcano across the European skies. According to The International Air Transport Association, the ash crisis led to the cancellation of over 100,000 flights and cost the world's airlines an estimated 1.7 billion dollars.

While many countries including England, Germany, Switzerland and Ireland were negatively affected by the volcano, Iceland unfortunately received the brunt of it. So as I said before, it appears that being an Icelander isn't always very advantageous. Or is it?

If we were to look at the situation creatively, a unique strategic marketing advantage becomes apparent. It would appear that Iceland is actually sitting on a lava-erupting, ash-spewing, cash-generating gold mine! In fact all they need to do is learn from the folks in the Congo...

A fascinating article featured on MSNBC by an Associated Press reporter, Todd Pitman, highlighted the ingenuity of a large town in the Eastern Congo known as Goma. The town is situated at the base of a live volcano called Mount Nyiragongo; it is considered to be one of Africa's most active and dangerous volcanoes.

Nyiragongo's lava is notoriously fluid and it can move at speeds up to 60 miles per hour downhill, with little warning. It's the precise thing you'd want to run away from as fast as you possibly can, right?

But instead of running away from it, local authorities are embracing it with open arms and transforming it into a one-of-a-kind tourist attraction. According to Mr. Pitman, authorities are hoping volcano tourism will provide vital new revenue, and help project a positive new image for the region. At one point, many hundreds — mainly Goma-based foreign aid workers — paid $200 each to climb the summit.

And that's just the beginning.

Residents have capitalized on their proximity to the volcano by building new stores, entertainment centers and even a hotel built on rocks from the lava fields named – most appropriately – Lavastone.

While the Eyjafjallajökull volcano was obviously a terrible blow to the country of Iceland, perhaps Icelanders would have done well to take advantage of the publicity received by this incident and market it to their advantage – as a unique tourist attraction that would boost tourism, attract foreign visitors and, most importantly, generate serious cash...all thanks to some clever marketing.

True, you may not view this as a potential family vacation. No explanation necessary...I perfectly understand. But believe it or not, there are folks out there who absolutely thrive on adventure and would like nothing more than to poke their noses over the rim of a steaming volcano and inhale the fresh scent of hot, molten lava. It's just a matter of knowing who the target markets are and getting the message out to them.

In all, while your business or organization doesn't have to deal with exploding volcanoes (or at least I would hope not), events will sometimes occur that may appear disastrous. However, by presenting them with proper marketing they can be presented to the public in a favorable and profitable light.

So next time you think something is about to erupt, take a deep breath and remember this marketing article about the erupting volcano – and just like the gushing lava streams, let the profits begin to flow.

BOTTOM LINE ACTION STEP:

What looks like an inherently bad thing, can turn out to be a marketing windfall. Look at all the black clouds and see if you can find the silver lining – then create a marketing initiative to turn it into gold.

PROCEED
with SPEED

Healthy competition is good for any business because it forces you to keep sharp and stay focused. But name and brand recognition is contingent upon putting distance between you and your competition. To accomplish that, dash out of the starting block and don't look back.

Most of us probably remember the fable about the plodding tortoise that beat the speedy hare in a race. The moral of the fable was that slow and steady wins the race.

Alas, this is only a fable. In real life, another race with great consequences is the presidential primaries. The first two ballots are held in Iowa and New Hampshire, as is customary. Even though they are two of the smallest states in the union, candidates from both parties spend a disproportionate amount of time and money, as winning these early races have proven to give a candidate momentum that becomes insurmountable.

The grassy plains of Iowa and the granite state of New Hampshire are stepping stones to the White House. Since 1972, Bill Clinton was the only man who lost both states and still got elected president. For New Hampshire itself, the money the candidates spend there is such a boon to them that the legislature passed a law that if any other state ever schedules its primary before New Hampshire's, then New Hampshire will simply reschedule theirs to an earlier date. There's no such thing as beating New Hampshire to the punch.

We can learn an important lesson about the importance of coming in first and getting off to a fast start. Recently, someone wrote me with a really outstanding idea, but one of his first questions was what could he do to protect it and make sure no one copied it?

This is an excellent question. Of course, one should always seek qualified legal advice to see what aspects of an idea can be copyrighted, patented or trademarked. However, since most forms of expression do not qualify for such protection, there is only one sure-fire way to ensure that your idea will remain yours and yours alone. Beat them to it with your great idea.

Establishing early momentum and emerging as the frontrunner in the public's mind is the crucial element of any marketing and advertising strategy. Barack Obama's win in the 2008 Iowa caucus, even as everyone assumed that Hillary Clinton was a cinch to get the nomination, knocked her off of her perch and established him as the frontrunner giving him and his campaign a giant confidence boost. People like to associate themselves with the frontrunner. Just as a winning candidate draws bigger crowds in the next primary state, a winning product or idea draws buyers and customers and discourages and disheartens the competition.

If you come up with a marketing or advertising concept, the best way to ensure that it sticks to you and no one copies it is to embark upon an aggressive campaign and blast it out there at full force.

Nike serves as a great example. In 1988, Nike devised their "Just Do It" campaign to increase its share of the domestic sport-shoe business. Over the next 10 years, their market share rose from 18% to 43%, and sales skyrocketed from $877 million worldwide to $9.2 billion. Unlike the hare, Nike never became complacent. You can still order Nike tee-shirts with the "Just Do It" slogan and Nike's revenues are many billions of dollars. By the way, it wasn't the slogan alone that did it for them. It was the $300 million they spent on the campaign that just did it. No one else has caught them since.

By the way, there is an updated version of the tortoise and the hare fable making the rounds at marketing schools. Disappointed at his loss, the hare conducted a root cause analysis. He realized he lost the race due to overconfidence, carelessness and laxity. He challenged the tortoise to a return match. The tortoise agreed. This time, the hare went all out and ran without stopping from start to finish. The rabbit pulled one "out of the hat" and won!

BOTTOM LINE ACTION STEP:
Establish your position early and proceed with speed!

57? 250? ... WHAT'S _your_ "MAGIC" NUMBER?

Do you have a magic number? Mr. Wang Ding of Guangzhou, China does.

According to an article in The New York Times, Mr. Ding paid $6,750 for a license plate with the numbers "888" in them – numerals considered to be magical in the Chinese culture.

Yeah, you read that right – $6,750. To put things into perspective, the price paid for his car's license plate was almost 20 times what a typical Chinese farmer earns in a year! While others would have probably spent that huge chunk of change on a Hawaiian vacation, or a new car, Mr. Ding felt it necessary to spend it on his favorite magic number for the license plate on his car.

What this guy did is his own business. However, in the business world, using a magic number can play a very important role in branding your message. Just ask the Heinz Ketchup Company. They ran a memorable advertising campaign based on the number "57" that is still considered one of the cleverest marketing strategies ever.

While riding a New York City train in 1896, founder Henry Heinz saw a billboard sign advertising 21 styles of shoes, which he thought was an intriguing marketing tactic. Although Heinz was manufacturing over 60 products at the time, Mr. Heinz instituted "57" as his company's "magic" number and began using the slogan "57 Varieties" in all his advertising literature. The concept was wildly popular with consumers and the distinct number of 57 remained in their heads when shopping for condiment products.

Today, over 100 years later, the company has more than 5,700 products and no longer uses the "57 Varieties" advertising campaign that originally helped the brand grow into an international conglomerate. However, as a tribute to the magic number that helped them rise to prominence, proudly emblazoned on every Heinz ketchup bottle till this very day is Mr. Heinz's magical number: 57.

How about Avis Rental Car's magic number? When advertising legend Bill Bernbach launched the now-famous Avis campaign, he used the power of a number – 2 – to illustrate that the company was second behind Hertz and had to try harder to please clients. While the executives at Avis may not have considered it to be a lucky number at first (after all, who wants to admit that they're not *numero uno*?) once the campaign generated millions of dollars in profits and increased Avis' market share, it's safe to assume they all started wearing the number 2 on their key chains!

The reality is, numbers can actually help position a product and serve as a memorable sales pitch to consumers. American Airlines uses numbers to tout its image as one of the world's largest airlines by stressing the fact that it serves over 250 cities in 40 different countries. Listerine highlights its ability to kill *millions* of germs on contact. And Bud Light beer points to its numerical lack of calories – *zero* – to show why the product is beneficial for those trying to keep their weight down.

In essence, numbers are very important for accountants, actuaries – and your corporate marketing efforts!

Does your company service an impressive amount of customers? Tout the fact in your ads (*"Over 150,000 happy mouths have enjoyed our delicious hamburgers!"*). Selling large numbers of certain products? Be sure to note the fact at in-store displays (*"Heads up – we've sold over 3 million hats to date!"*). Even non-profit organizations have impressive numerical statistics to boast about. Two examples are, *"468 children have been saved from malnutrition this past year,"* or *"over 63 classes given each week."*

By using the power of numbers to emphasize the benefits of your product, company or organization, you are practically stamping an indelible, hard-hitting marketing fact into potential customers' heads, hearts and most importantly, wallets.

BOTTOM LINE ACTION STEP:

Try to think of numbers you can use in your ads. Because as you can see, numbers are more than just magical – they're profitable too!

 **PICTURE PERFECT!**

We all have certain memorable images buried deep within the recesses of our minds.

For the older generation, it may be the carnage at Pearl Harbor or the terrible assassination of President John F. Kennedy. For the younger generation, it may be the Berlin Wall toppling down or the horrific and tragic events of 9/11. Regardless of how long ago the events took place, the images relating to it will never be forgotten.

We also carry personal images within our minds at all times. It can be of our graduation, wedding day or the birth of a child. The images of these momentous occasions are burnt clearly into our cerebral cortex and will always remain vivid and fresh.

In fact, when somebody just happens to mention the word "wedding day," you may subconsciously envision yourself standing next to your spouse worrying about whether someone actually has the ring.

As you can see – and as psychologists and scientists have undoubtedly proven – the powers of images are tremendous. A memorable image can, in some ways, give over more information than an entire set of oversized encyclopedias.

Dr. Gerard J. Tellis, a noted Professor of Marketing at the USC Marshall School of Business wrote a fascinating book titled: Effective Advertising; Understanding When, How And Why Advertising Works (a must read for anybody interested in the delicate intricacies of marketing). In the book, Dr. Tellis highlights the many prominent campaigns that have used memorable images to advance their agenda.

One such marketing campaign involved an organization dedicated to preventing cruelty to animals. When they launched a campaign against the Gillette company, depicting how animals were being used in laboratory experiments for product testing, images were crucial for the campaign's success. The organization posted ghastly photos of cute-looking animals being subjected to tortuous experiments, prompting many to boycott Gillette's products.

When a public outcry started to erupt, Gillette responded to the organization's attention-grabbing and memorable ads with statistical figures showing that its laboratory tests conformed to federal regulations, and were designed to inflict very little pain. However, despite Gillette's best efforts, their informative statistics just didn't seem to pacify the public. And here's why.

When you pit reason (e.g. the statistical figures released by Gillette) against emotion (e.g. haunting images of little animals tortured in a laboratory), emotion will always win. We all know that horrifying images will linger in people's minds, causing them to toss and turn uncomfortably at night. Number-crunching statistics may be accurate, but they don't do much in terms of jostling people out of their nightly sleep routines.

In all, as a direct result of that organization's image-oriented ads, many companies no longer use animals for product research.

Therefore, it is imperative that organizations and institutions liberally spread images throughout their marketing materials.

That angelic, special needs child reading a book; the poor, impoverished child with deep, sunken eyes and a worried expression; and the lonely, old woman staring blankly ahead, bereft of companionship and hope. These images speak volumes. They convey the powerful and memorable message that twenty-five long paragraphs in Times New Roman font cannot.

Organizations too (as well as for-profit companies), should create images that project the entity's mission and message. When done properly, the mere mention of the entity's name should trigger an instant recollection of an image relating to the organization.

For example, in the aftermath of Hurricane Katrina in 2005, the American Red Cross had powerful advertisements featuring people affected by the hurricane.

They showed photos of frightened children in shelters; once booming neighborhoods completely destroyed; and whole families left with no place to go. These harrowing images touched people's hearts – and they opened their wallets. According to a September 25, 2005 article in the Los Angeles Times, in the wake of Hurricane Katrina, the American Red Cross raised an astonishing 2 billion dollars!

While you may not necessarily expect the same results for your organization or institution, you could – and should – utilize the same image-oriented marketing tactics to leave potential donors with a lasting visual picture of what you do.

SO, WHAT'S THE BOTTOM LINE?

So whether you're making a new brochure, sending out your quarterly newsletter or doing a direct mail campaign, be sure to load up your camera with a 4 GB memory card and start snapping away. Or better yet, hire a professional photographer who will be able to capture the moment that will "speak a thousand words!"

BOTTOM LINE ACTION STEP:

Use pictures to your advantage to get your message out with visual emotional impact.

KODAK MOMENTS

Did you ever collect baseball cards as a child?

Yes, you know what I am referring to. Those glossy, colorful cards adorned with the faces of baseball heroes and their team on the front and a synopsis of their statistics and a brief bio on the back. Hours of young boys' lives were spent analyzing those cards and trying to decide which ones were worth trading.

But did you ever wonder how those photos came to be?

Well, in a large part, the credit for all these photos goes to a gentleman from Rochester, New York named George Eastman. Inventor, marketer and businessman, Mr. Eastman revolutionized the world of photography by coming up with the concept of camera film. In 1892 he opened a camera company called (maybe you have heard of it?) Kodak, which went by the memorable slogan: "You press the button, we do the rest!"

As any marketer can tell you, the name of a business can sometimes make it or break it. And Mr. Eastman knew that quite well. There was quite a bit of marketing thought that went into the Kodak name.

According to Wikipedia, the letter "K" had been a favorite of Eastman's. He felt it was a strong, incisive sort of letter. Eastman and his mother devised the name Kodak with an anagram set. He used three principal concepts to create the name: it had to be short, it could not be mispronounced, and it could not resemble anything else or be associated with anything other than itself – hence the name Kodak!

As the popularity of this new concept called "film" grew, other camera film companies began sprouting up and began affecting Kodak's sales, Mr. Eastman – ever the savvy marketer – realized that a memorable, hard-hitting advertising campaign was needed to keep sales up and the Kodak brand at the top of the market.

A campaign was launched featuring ads with photos of people doing everyday things. Parents spending time with their children; a baby taking his first step; families joining together at celebrations; friends enjoying each others company, and so on. The tag line that was used for this advertising campaign was, "These are the moments. Kodak moments."

A deceivingly simple concept, yet one that focused on what Kodak enabled people to do: capture precious, memorable and unforgettable moments forever.

The millennials may be too young to remember this, but the advertising campaign was a tremendous success and further solidified Kodak's position as the industry leader, into the beginning of the 21st Century. But another interesting phenomenon arose; one that added Kodak's brand name into the American lexicon.

The campaign tag line "Kodak moment" was transformed into an everyday, common expression. A person seeing a memorable scene would say, "Oh look, that's such a Kodak moment!" Consumers automatically began associating memorable events, occasions or places with the Kodak brand. Indeed, the power of an effective adverting campaign.

But smart marketing isn't just about selling film – it's about selling through a photo as well. Marketing guru Alan Rosenspan, utilized the power of photography to sell a diet drink called Ultra Slim. He posted ads showing a before and after picture of somebody who lost weight and wrote the following headline in the ad: "Send us your photo... we'll take off the weight."

The ad encouraged consumers to send a photo of themselves to Ultra Slim. A computer generated photo of the consumer – thin, in shape and at their desired weight – would be sent back, illustrating how the consumer would look after drinking a monthly regimen of Ultra Slim's diet drink. Needless to say, after seeing their "photo" and realizing how they could actually appear in real life, people began buying bottles of Ultra Slim by the pound!

So whether you're a young boy trading baseball cards, or just feeling good looking at a photo of yourself at your desired weight, keep one thing in mind – this is all possible due to the tremendous power of effective marketing!

BOTTOM LINE ACTION STEP:

Sometimes the simplest concept can turn into the greatest most effective marketing campaign. Think of people's real life activities and dreams and incorporate them into your campaign.

A BEHIND THE SCENES LOOK *at* POLITICAL MARKETING

It's the same every year. November rolls around and millions of Americans turn out on Election Day to vote in local, state, and even federal elections. Americans shuffle into the voting booth and choose their preferred political candidates with the push of a lever, or the punch of a chad.

And you all know what that means.

Massive political advertising campaigns. Cars with loudspeakers blaring, slowly traipsing through New York's diverse neighborhoods proclaiming in English, Spanish, Chinese and other unintelligible languages whom to vote for. Lampposts decorated with mounds of colorful election posters; red, white and blue political bumper stickers clinging for dear life onto every street sign, fire hydrant and billboard in sight. Every other radio and television ad ending with "This message was paid for by Candidate X for office."

Alas, the voters themselves have taken the time to make their way into the polling stations – often a public school gymnasium or local fire station – and have eagerly performed their civic duty.

But while the actual voting process lasts for a mere few minutes, the events leading up to Election Day have been in the works for months...or even years!

The various marketing materials used in a political campaign didn't just appear overnight. Political analysts and marketing consultants spent weeks debating over the color, language and even sizes. Mailings were nitpicked at, revised, and then nitpicked at some more. The location of every campaign billboard was taken into consideration along with the surrounding neighborhood's ethnic makeup and population.

Thousands of hours, infinite amounts of manpower and millions of dollars were spent leading up to Election Day – and as the candidates sincerely hope, were not in vain.

Some election campaigns are designed to strike a chord in people's hearts and are often widely received throughout. One such example is Ronald Reagan's "It's morning in America again" presidential campaign. After the Carter administration's disappointing tenure consisting mostly of oil embargoes, terrorist attacks, global humiliation and national malaise, President Reagan single-handedly transformed the United States of America back into the prosperous, respected nation it really was.

Therefore, when running for re-election, Reagan used the "Morning again" theme to illustrate how things were indeed brighter for the American people. The economy was robust, the nation strong and there were positive opportunities scattered all across the horizon.

In many of Reagan's presidential campaign ads, powerful photos were used to bring the point home. Images featured a farmer plowing his bushy wheat field as the sun slowly rose behind him; smartly-dressed businesspeople walking confidentially to their workplaces; children happily frolicking together with their parents in comfort and safety as the sun shines brightly upon them, with the reassuring knowledge that their country is secure.

These poignant, moving images reached across to and touched the heart of many American voters – and ultimately, landed Ronald Reagan back in the White House for another four productive years.

While the Reagan campaign focused on the positive by accentuating a warm feeling of serenity that members of every political party were able to relate to, some prominent political campaigns have utilized the "shock and awe" approach to galvanize legions of dedicated supporters – and create droves of staunch opponents.

For example, Barack Obama's presidential "Campaign for Change" electrified the Democratic Party and brought an unprecedented amount of voters to the polls.

Utilizing a full array of print, digital and online media, the Obama campaign's message of change resonated with many war-weary and recession-plagued Americans.

Of course, not all political campaigns have been run on a platform of prosperity or change. According to an article in The Oakland Tribune, a candidate in the Alameda, California mayoral race actually included a real clown. Kenny Kahn – known professionally as Kenny the Clown – hoped to juggle his way into the City Hall by adapting a marketing slogan used for his clown business to his political campaign. The catchy jingle? "We take being silly very seriously!" It's an idea, Kahn said, which fit his political campaign very nicely.

BOTTOM LINE ACTION STEP:

Create a political campaign strategy designed to touch the heart and soul of voters.

3 TRICKS *in* GETTING FREE PUBLICITY

How does a business get its message out to the public?

Traditionally, various forms of media such as advertisements in newspapers and direct mailings have been used. As of late, e-mail marketing, web banners, Google AdWords, and other forms of internet marketing have proven quite effective – especially for internet-based businesses. But for the purpose of this article, we'll focus on some creative entrepreneurs who marketed their businesses with... menorahs!

According to PR Newswire, an upscale Manhattan florist has come up with a novel way to ply their trade by creating the world's first-ever floral menorah.

The six-foot tall, rose-bedecked menorah was so remarkable that New York's Mayor, at that time, Mike Bloomberg, displayed it as the centerpiece at his annual Hanukkah party where it generated tremendous publicity for the florist. More than just a unique way to celebrate a festival, this menorah proves that clever marketing ideas really do come in all shapes, sizes and scents!

Alternatively, as noted in The New York Times, two Jewish physics students created an oversized electric menorah powered by (are you ready for this one?) a miniature wind turbine! As self-described proponents of alternative energy, the eco-friendly creation definitely fit in with their message of sustainable power awareness.

Remember FAO Schwartz, the legendary Manhattan toy store that we'd go to for our holiday presents as kids? Well, perhaps they would be interested in housing the world's largest LEGO menorah as a way of attracting more Jewish customers. Stephen Schwartz, a renowned architect, utilized his skills to design and construct a mammoth menorah made from LEGO toys. Talk about building a great reputation via out-of-the-box marketing techniques!

In 2005, the world's largest balloon menorah was formed. In 2006, the world's largest edible menorah replete with chocolate and jelly donut building materials was created. And of course, The Big Apple is the home to the world's biggest menorah (as certified by the Guinness Book of World Records), soaring high in midtown Manhattan at Grand Army Plaza on Central Park South.

All these different menorahs have been used as marketing tools for reaching out to the public with specific messages and gaining publicity. While your business doesn't have to use a menorah to help sustain its brand, keep in mind that there are many ways to generate publicity for your company, business or organization.

Here are set of tried-and-true rules that I call: *The 3 Ways To Get Absolutely Free Publicity.*

RULE # 1 – IT'S ALL ABOUT PROMOTIONS!

A California restaurant created a promotional event called the "We Like Baldies Day" where all balding men who came into the restaurant ate for free. The press got wind of the interesting story and it landed on the front page of a local newspaper.

Meanwhile, there were some patrons blessed with full heads of hair who didn't qualify for the promotion. They sent letters to the newspaper complaining about the perceived discrimination and raised a ruckus. Of course, the press covered that as well. Finally, after generating two newspapers' worth of publicity, the restaurant announced a special promotion for men that had full heads of hair. Naturally, the press publicized this as well.

So at the day's end, this restaurant garnered tremendous free publicity... all thanks to a clever promotion!

RULE # 2 – TAKE YOUR MESSAGE TO THE PODIUM!

Public speaking engagements can be awkward for some – and quite lucrative for others. If you have a message to get out, be sure to say it loudly.

An acquaintance of mine, used to travel the globe tracking down obscure and antique Jewish books. He was often invited as a guest lecturer at large events where he regaled the crowds with his fascinating adventures. Aside from wowing the crowd with his impressive discoveries, he inevitably found clients who wished to purchase copies of these rare Judaic manuscripts.

Ahh, the power of successfully marketing a product via public speaking!

RULE # 3 – CHOOSE A GOOD CAUSE!

Traditionally known as Cause Marketing, it involves aligning your entity with a noteworthy organization or charity.

For example, I recall a number of years ago, a business in New York placed ads in the papers stating that it was donating a percentage of profits to a Volunteer Ambulance Corps. Aside from generating tremendous goodwill with members of this volunteer ambulance organization (and quite possibly, having many of them become loyal customers), he also ended up getting great press coverage in the papers about his business.

In essence, a good cause can produce great results!

BOTTOM LINE ACTION STEP:

Be creative in your approach to getting free publicity.

FUNDRAISING *by* THE BOOK

Remembering birthdays and important anniversaries is not only important for marital harmony, it also can bring payoffs for something else near and dear to your heart – your non-profit organization. Learn how to attain new fundraising records from your milestone events.

Do the numbers 10, 18, 25, 36, 50 mean anything to you?

While at first glance it could be a quarterback calling plays or maybe a good stab at next week's winning lottery numbers, these numbers are actually vastly more meaningful.

Almost every school or non-profit organization is just a few years away from an important milestone anniversary that should be leveraged to motivate donors and raise more money. Anniversary campaigns will always re-energize your existing corps of dedicated fund raisers by providing them with new and promising opportunities to generate awareness for their cause.

Prior to beginning an anniversary campaign, one should start thinking about developing a concept, message and campaign time line and the accompanying marketing materials you will need to be successful – from save the date cards and newsletters to "memento" publications.

Perhaps you may have seen, one or more of the many books that Bottom Line Marketing Group published on behalf of venerable organizations commemorating their milestone anniversaries. No other memento offers a better way to position and brand a school or organization and generate awareness of their day to day work and long term impact.

I first began to appreciate the power of the book in my formative working years when I had the privilege to gain valuable experience at ArtScroll/Mesorah, where I assisted in putting out more than 100 books. There are few things more inspirational, prestigious and permanent than a stunning, full color, hardcover book that you can use to increase your fundraising directly and indirectly in the following ways:

- **Recognize your founders with a "Founder's Circle" feature**
- **Make chapters available for dedication**
- **Recognize honorees and top donors**
- **Galvanize donors, alumni and community members, etc.**

This is not to say that everyone will or should produce such a book. Obviously, there are also the costs to consider. While the overall costs might seem expensive, many times clients have had their campaigns sponsored by a donor who wishes to see the organization's prominence documented in a permanent way.

BOTTOM LINE ACTION STEP:
Think big! Book greater revenues by considering a book of your own!

A LESSON IN MARKETING *from* THE FEDS

Not all of us are blessed to sell bread or ice cream that everyone must buy or can't live without. Sometimes our goods or services are a "harder sell," but we can make our job easier by placing our customers in the driver's seat and making their priorities ours.

America is world-renowned for its marketing genius and sometimes, even our own federal government leads the way.

For several years, the Environmental Protection Agency (EPA) has been urging people to conserve energy – not by sleeping later, or by turning their clocks forward at the end of the month – but by choosing cleaner, more fuel efficient transportation options.

The EPA knew it would be a hard-sell to change habits among the nation's leading transportation companies and shippers. A secondary goal was to convince individual consumers to buy "green" cars instead of gas-slurping SUVs. So, a few years ago, the EPA embarked upon a marketing campaign which they called – SmartWay – the smart way to save fuel, money and the environment.

Why did they choose this slogan? Obviously, they needed to motivate people to climb on board. Sure, everyone wants to breathe cleaner air, and saving fuel sounds praiseworthy, but how do you make it meaningful? By telling your target audience that it will save them money! Now we start firing on all cylinders. Is there anyone you know who doesn't love to save money?

Even though the EPA's primary goal was to save the environment, they understood that you have to market the benefits to the customer, and get on their wavelength. Maybe a handful of environmentally conscious people would have signed up for a program to save the environment but if you make the pitch saving money, then everyone gets on board, because we all pay through the teeth for fuel.

The results of the EPA campaign speak for itself. Major corporations that ship freight nationwide and worldwide, like UPS, PepsiCo, Home Depot and Kraft Foods, were among the thousands that signed up for SmartWay's Transport Partnership. By 2012, SmartWay was saving America 150 million barrels of oil a year. At over $100 a barrel, that's more than $15 billion in savings. Wouldn't you rather have that kind of cash in your pocket than send it overseas for imported oil?

You don't need to save or make billions when devising your own marketing campaign. You can be just as successful on your own scale, as long as you devise your own smart way. Think carefully about the hot button issue for your customers or clients. If you are selling home security, your system may be laden with the latest high tech gizmos, and that's worth mentioning, but your priority "pitch" has to be how your product keeps people feeling safe and secure. If you're a travel agency, the hotel room with the chocolates placed on the pillow is nice, (as long as they kept the air conditioning on after they left them there), but the vacationer's priority is rest and relaxation.

There's one more important point to get across. You have to make people feel good about their decision to change their habits or to part with their money.

The EPA accomplished this by telling people that signing up for SmartWay will "reflect well on you." This doesn't mean that you look good in green. The EPA is giving you an ego massage. Partner with us and you will become more important. That ego boost is nice when you're sitting low to the road in a Chevy Volt instead of tall in the saddle in a Suburban.

By the way, SmartWay applied their smarts in more ways than one. As one might expect from a government agency, they are an equal opportunity media employer. SmartWay used radio, television, print, internet, e-mail and even RSS feeds to drive their message home. There's nothing like a comprehensive, diversified campaign to ensure the greatest exposure to your target market.

BOTTOM LINE ACTION STEP:

Devise a "priority pitch" and drive that point home.

SUSTAINING
your **BUSINESS**
Customer Retention

> *The customer is why you go to work.*
> *If they go away, you do, too.*
>
> — David Haverford

UNDERSTANDING "CUSTOMER RETENTION"

Here's a rather tricky question:

You are the proud owner of a thriving business with lots of customers. Like every other entrepreneur, you want to continue increasing your sales and profits. How should you go about doing this?

   A. Obtain targeted mailing lists of potential clients and send out postcards offering them a 10% discount on their first purchase.

   B. Send an e-mail blast to your existing client-base thanking them for their business and notifying them of an upcoming sale.

   C. Blast your favorite song on your iPhone and sing it at the top of your lungs (hey, if it won't attract customers, at least it'll put you in a good mood!)

Okay, we all know that option C isn't much of an option (unless you operate an amusement park!); that leaves us with the first two. But before you read any further, close your eyes and decide which one you'd choose...

Here's the answer: If you chose both, you're a marketing genius!

Both of those methods have much merit and, depending on the circumstances, can be used by themselves, with each other or intertwined with other marketing tactics. In the marketing world they are referred to as *lead generation* and *customer retention*.

Obtaining targeted mailing lists of potential clients falls into the *lead generation* category. This involves generating the interest of prospective customers about your company. It can prove to be expensive and time-consuming, as it requires finding and educating complete strangers about the services and/or products that your company offers.

Sending an e-mail blast to your existing client-base and expressing your thanks to them falls into the *customer retention* category. This is what a company undertakes in order to reduce customer defections and retain their patronage. The process begins with the first contact a company has with its customer and continues throughout the entire lifetime of a relationship – which will hopefully last for many, many years. It is often easier to embark on this route as customers are already familiar with your company and view it in a positive frame of mind.

Who should use these marketing methods? Every business.

Here's an example about how a company boosted their *customer retention* techniques – and significantly boosted profits.

A while back, the owner of a car leasing company came to me wanting to run an advertising campaign. As we discussed his options, I asked him who this campaign was geared toward. He replied that the ads were meant to attract new clients.

"Alright," I said, "but what about your existing clients? What are you doing to keep them on board?" He looked at me incredulously. "You mean I should do marketing just for existing clients? But they already know about me!"

He clearly didn't understand that just because clients knew about him, didn't guarantee that they would return to him for their next lease. They had to be reminded and encouraged to do so. I immediately advised him to send out mailings to every client that had a lease ending within the next 90 days. The letter thanked the client for their valued business and served as a pitch about new leases available. The marketing plan actually called for mailing 3 postcards within those 90 days – 4 weeks apart.

Additionally, I advised him to send a personalized thank you note to each client who had just signed a new lease with him. The response he received after doing so was tremendous and he quickly realized the importance of *customer retention.*

Customer retention is a concept that must be taken very seriously. In fact, twice annually, I make it a point of sending out a personalized letter to each and every client, thanking them for their business. Each letter has a handwritten comment at the bottom to show that it really is personalized; adding that personal touch on a thank you note to show customers your appreciation for their business is priceless.

Another idea is to take advantage of e-mail marketing to keep clients updated on the latest happenings at your company. Bottom Line sends out monthly e-newsletters to inform and yes, even entertain clients, keeping the bond strong. While e-mail can also serve as a form of *lead generation,* the real power of e-mail marketing is to your current client base and list of contacts – *customer retention.*

BOTTOM LINE ACTION STEP:

Write a personal thank you note to your #1 client, today!

"CUSTOMER RETENTION" TIPS & TECHNIQUES

As a rule, people (unfortunately) often forget things; that includes businesses in their database, and clients forgetting about a business that they have patronized in the past. Precisely, that is why customer retention is so important – every company must have a marketing method in place in order to remind past and current clients of the services previously provided for them...and that your company is available to offer that service for them in the future.

A common misconception is that customer retention tactics are only for certain entities doing lots of repeat business, such as supermarkets and restaurants. After all, why would a catering hall, for example, busy themselves with sending out a thoughtful thank you card and ongoing communication to a client who just had a wedding in their venue? The event is over, there seems to be no future opportunity from this client...no more business to be had.

Or is that so?

Let's examine the situation closely. The catering hall was presumably hired by the bride and groom and/or their parents. It's fair to say that these people know others who are also of marriageable age. At some future point, a conversation is going to take place about a couple getting engaged. Naturally, there is a good chance that a discussion about potential venues for the wedding will then occur!

Now, if the caterer had sent a beautiful thank you card, and kept in touch with this past client long after the wedding, undoubtedly, the catering hall would be referred along with glowing accolades!

You see, despite the fact that the client in our story got married and no longer need the catering hall's services, there is a very good chance that others they know will need one. And it's precisely through customer retention techniques that will enable this catering establishment to be kept in the forefront of a past client's mind.

According to nearly every business study ever done, all statistics show that it's more expensive to acquire a new client than it is to retain an existing one. In most cases, your past clients are the ones most likely to be future purchasers; they've already shown they want your service or product and are willing to pay for it. And even in our case above, when a vendor would no longer be needed by a client, there is still great opportunity from that client as a source for valuable referrals.

Here are 6 proven tips and techniques that will help beef up your customer retention efforts, regardless of your profession or industry:

1. **CONTACT YOUR TOP CLIENTS REGULARLY!**
    Make a list of your top 25 clients. Personally call or mail something to them every few months. Even better, visit them!

2. **KEEP YOUR NAME IN FRONT OF ALL YOUR CLIENTS!**
    Mail a personal note at least twice a year. Send out a newsletter with updated information about your products or services quarterly. Send a monthly e-mail update.

3. **ADVERTISE!**

   Advertising regularly is a sure way to remain in your clients mind, as well as generate new leads.

4. **MAKE THEM REMEMBER YOU!**

   Your corporate name and logo dangling in front of clients on a daily basis – like on their key rings, pens, post-it notes, and the like – continuously remind them of your company.

5. **OFFER YOUR CURRENT CLIENTS SPECIAL DEALS!**

   This particular suggestion applies especially to the B to C retail world. Retailers mail catalogs, coupons and offers on a postcard or via e-mail to their client database as a great way of getting them back into their store.

6. **SURPRISE THEM!**

   Do something special and unexpected for some of your top clients. Send them a small gift. Add something extra to their order. As my good friend, Jonathan Gassman likes to put it, "Show 'em some love!"

The bottom line? Communicate, communicate and communicate! Businesses often take their clients for granted – don't be one of them! Ask your clients what they need and want. Listen to their ideas, comments and yes, even complaints. When clients see that you're genuinely interested in them, they will most certainly reciprocate and be interested in patronizing your business as well. Make them want to do business with you again. And again. And again.

BOTTOM LINE ACTION STEP:

Your past clients are most likely to be your future customers.

"CUSTOMER RETENTION" CASE STUDIES

They say that it's difficult to understand somebody else until you've been in their shoes.

Well then, when it comes to improving customer retention, we should all try to stand in the footwear of the trendsetting online shoe store, Zappos.com.

With millions of satisfied customers, the Nevada-based online shoe retailer has doubled its sales nearly every year since 1999. How did they accomplish that? All agree: it was primarily on their plethora of successful customer retention techniques. They genuinely back up their tag line, Powered by Service™.

According to an article in CNN Money, Zappos' operating philosophy is based on a long-term customer-retention strategy. On any given day, 65 percent of Zappos shoppers are repeat customers.

Helpful features like 24 hour customer service and a 365 day return-policy have ensured that Zappos shoppers walk away happy (no pun intended) and come back again for their next shoe shopping experience.

If a customer likes their purchase, that's great. If not, they can ship it back at absolutely no cost – and a huge inventory almost guarantees they'll find something else to wear.

To further illustrate how important customer retention is to Zappos, at one point they eliminated drop shipping items to customers (which actually produced 25% of Zappos revenue) because every so often, a few customers would find out their purchased item was actually out of stock. The customer would obviously be quite upset, create a lot of negative word of mouth, and not easily return. Zappos therefore walked away from it and only sells footwear stocked in its oversized warehouse because they knew it was important to be true to their brand and continuously boost customer retention levels.

The company also sends existing customers e-mails detailing upcoming sales, specials and events, putting them in the know before the general public and enticing Zappos shoppers to come back for more deals.

But it's not *only* a company that has put customer retention at the forefront of their marketing plan.

BankTech Magazine reports that financial institutions are adding functionality to their ATMs in an effort to improve the customer experience and boost retention.

J.P. Morgan Chase added check scanners to their ATMs so that the machines can accept checks without envelopes and issue receipts, more closely matching the experience of a teller window.

Bank of America converted all 18,000 of its automated teller machines into "talking ATMs" equipped with audio equipment and headphones so that customers can speak live with a bank representative while using the machines.

And when it comes to the auto industry, they've really kicked up the horsepower on customer retention techniques. Take Subaru, for example.

The car company invested millions to accurately guarantee that customers were enjoying the brand, starting with the sales showroom. Thanks to advanced tracking technology, the company can tell which salesperson at a dealership is turning customers off from buying a vehicle and what that person is doing that is causing this to happen. Subaru can also measure how retention rates are trending for specific target markets and track satisfaction levels for specific customers.

Does it work? You bet!

For instance, most Subaru cars weren't even eligible for the U.S. government's *Cash for Clunkers* program a few years back, yet Subaru sold around 17,000 of their few eligible vehicles through the program during that time. Impressive indeed.

Bottom line?

The point is that customer retention techniques – when properly implemented – do work, do have customers returning for more and most certainly do increase profits. Or as Zappos would say: "It's a shoe-in!"

BOTTOM LINE ACTION STEP:
Tune in to the "wants and needs" of your customers.

CUSTOMER RETENTION: *Loyalty* PROGRAMS

When it comes to aviation firsts during the year of 1981, most history books focus on the creation of the famous Boeing 767 jetliner and how it helped revolutionize modern air travel. But very few mention a feat equally as impressive – at least from a marketing perspective – that helped revolutionize the overall airline industry.

In May of 1981, American Airlines launched the very first full-scale loyalty marketing program with their AAdvantage frequent flyer program. This revolutionary program was the first to reward "frequent fliers" with reward miles that could be accumulated and later redeemed for free travel.

The premise behind this concept was simple. Give customers a tangible incentive to come back – and they absolutely will. Needless to say, it worked. In fact, the AAdvantage program now boasts over 70 million active members.

Within a few years time, almost every airline in the industry had frequent flyer programs of their own, with the common goal of increasing customer retention.

But with time, things change. As such, having a loyalty program alone is no longer good enough. Companies must use their loyalty programs as springboards for introducing customers to other features and amenities as well. For example, why not utilize these programs to further educate customers about your brand and interact with them on a personal level?

Case in point: Southwest Airlines raised the bar in customer retention techniques by incorporating what they dub a "Vacation Destination Giveaway" in conjunction with the airline's Rapid Rewards frequent flyer program.

The program ran for an eight-week promotion. Members had a daily opportunity to answer Rapid Rewards trivia questions and play an instant-win game with prizes including Rapid Rewards credits and free round trip tickets. The promotion highlighted a specific Southwest destination each week.

In a press release, Ryan Green, Southwest's Director of Customer Loyalty said, "Our Vacation Destination Giveaway is a fun way for us to engage and educate our members about our breadth of service and our Rapid Rewards program." The giveaway featured eight of their 69 destinations and gave loyal members a chance to win a trip to go, see, and do.

In this case, Southwest reinforced their brand to customers and simultaneously educated them about all the destinations the airline travels to. Sure, the promotion may seem like fun and games (which it obviously was intended to be) to the customer. But the next time that customer needs an immediate flight to Fort Lauderdale, Florida, guess which airline they're probably going to make those reservations with...?!

As of late, some loyalty programs have developed a tarnished image due to the myriads of restrictions imposed by them regarding days of availability, seasonal eligibility, and off-peak times. Apparently, the companies making all these rules for their loyalty programs seem to have forgotten the original point of these programs: to retain customers by having them come back again.

Placing severe restrictions on such loyalty programs merely turns the customer off and leaves them with a bad taste in their mouth.

Why not create a program that the customer actually feels good about? Let's take a look at the executives from the Marriott Hotel who figured out ways to impress clients rather than turn them away.

According to The Wall Street Journal, Marriott Hotel's guest loyalty program was once named "Best Frequent Guest Program" by the readers of Executive Travel magazine. Customers faced no restrictions with Marriott Rewards because there were no blackout dates and members could earn and redeem points at more than 3,200 Marriott International hotels around the world. Members could also redeem points for frequent flyer miles, cruises, car rentals, brand-name merchandise and more.

In other words, members could actually enjoy the brand, feel good about what the brand has done for them and continue using the services offered by the brand for years to come.

Flying high, staying comfortable and generating profits – now that's what successful customer retention is all about.

BOTTOM LINE ACTION STEP:

Implement a "loyalty" benefit program for your customers.

CUSTOMER RETENTION: OH MY...WHAT _not_ TO DO!

Generally, I patronize a barbershop shop near my home which is owned by a Russian fellow. However, for the past few months I was unable to use him due to "scheduling conflicts."

So when I went in to his barbershop for a haircut, I was sure he'd welcome me back with a smile and hello (and maybe even a bear hug!). Actually, I got a lot more than just a routine greeting.

"My friend," he began. "Where you be lately?"

"What is matter, you no like me no more?" he continued in his thick accent. "Why you go to other barbers? I tell you, I only give the best haircuts in Brooklyn. If you go to anybody else, you no look good. Mister, you only look nice if you come to me for haircut! You understand?"

Sounds too outrageous to be true?

Tell me about it! A friend of mine happened to be in the barbershop as well, and almost fell out of his chair in laughter while witnessing the unbelievable spectacle.

To be fair, on one hand I appreciated that my Russian barber remembered me and sincerely wanted to continue offering me his haircutting services.

On the other hand, I wish someone would teach him "a more tactful way" of letting me know that I was sorely missed. I mean, how in the world can a business owner "rank out" a customer – in front of a shop full of other customers no less! – and expect that client to return?

So in keeping with the series of "customer retention," here are some Do's and Don'ts to keep your customers coming back:

DO Acknowledge Your Customers –
From answering ringing office phones right away, to a simple "I'll be right with you" for customers waiting for assistance, acknowledging your customers immediately will definitely help boost your customer retention levels.

DO Know Your Customers –
Learn some information about the people you serve. Find out their full names and greet them by name whenever possible. Get birthday or anniversary information and offer them congratulations – or even send a card – around that time of year.

DO Ask Customers For Their Opinions –
It's always good to ask customers about their overall experience and what improvements they would like. They feel respected...and you'll get free feedback on how to improve operations even more.

DON'T Ask Customers Why They Haven't Patronized You Lately – You're not a KGB agent and your clients aren't prisoners. They have a right to go wherever they want. If you so badly want their patronage, focus on providing them with a first-class experience...and they'll be back for more.

DON'T Talk Negatively About The Competition – The best way to prove to customers that you're above the competition is by showing it through positive actions; not by bad mouthing the competitor down the block.

DON'T Insult Customers – Must I really explain why this is a major no-no?!

So while I don't know if my local Russian barber will be reading and implementing these simple, yet important, customer retention tips, I do hope that you will heed the message and create your own successful customer retention guidelines.

Try them and see the results for yourself...it'll make your company or business a cut above the rest.

BOTTOM LINE ACTION STEP:
Practice the art of genuine client interest...for great client retention.

CUSTOMER RETENTION: *The* POWER OF CUSTOMER SURVEYS

Do you constantly look for ways to generate more business? Well, have you ever polled your client-base to determine what new services or features your company can offer? Never underestimate the value and importance of customer surveys.

Surveys help businesses by revealing the satisfaction levels and preferences of their customers. A constant flow of customer feedback can help direct companies in making improvements that positively impact sales and profits. There are numerous methods for conducting surveys; some are extremely costly and others are surprisingly economical.

Focus groups and face-to-face interviews fall into the first category as they require significant manpower and time to sort through the overwhelming amount of data generated.

A phone survey offers some of the advantages of face-to-face interviews and focus groups without the additional cost involved (although nothing ever replaces face-to-face interaction).

Surveys sent to participants via direct mail have proven to be quite successful, as it allows the people being surveyed to think about their answers before writing them down, often resulting in more accurate and insightful feedback.

However, mailed surveys always face the risk of being discarded or not answered by the recipient. Therefore, it is imperative to grab the participant's attention with a complimentary coupon, free gift offer, or even the promise of something that will benefit them directly. Just like the biggest survey of them all – the U.S. Census Bureau – successfully did with their advertising campaign.

According to PRNewswire, The U.S. Census Bureau is being recognized by Mediaweek, a leading advertising industry trade publication, for its 2010 Census advertising campaign. The primary purpose of the Census' advertising efforts were to educate and motivate households to mail back their 2010 Census forms when they arrived in March — and more than 72 percent of America participated.

The Census sparked the interest of participants by showing that when they take 10 minutes to fill out the questionnaire, they help get their communities what they need for the next 10 years. For instance, one convincing headline they used on their mailings (and alternative advertising methods as well) asked, "If we don't know how many kids there are, how do we know how many classrooms we need?"

With a hard-hitting sales pitch like that, it's no wonder that Americans made it a priority to mail those forms back quickly and on-time.

Another popular survey method that has become almost ubiquitous when completing a shopping transaction online is e-mail and pop-up surveys. According to numerous studies, the response times and percentages of these surveys are quite high, and customers appreciate the ease and convenience.

Of course, surveys do more than just provide important feedback; they also create a bond between your company and the customer, helping involve them in your brand and your success.

For example, the Evenflo Savvy Parents Survey is the first in a series of polls that infant and juvenile product manufacturer, Evenflo, conducted to gauge the feelings of people and their everyday parenting dilemmas. The surveys were part of the "The Savvy Parents Guide", an online destination aimed at providing education, resources and a sense of community for parents in the know.

While parents benefitted by sharing common parenting concerns and possibly finding helpful solutions, Evenlo benefitted more by having their finger on the pulse of the parenting community, and in-turn, they created new products that addressed the problems and concerns faced by the modern-day parent.

But most of all, when that new product – the brainchild of the parents participating in Evenflo's survey – is launched, guess who will be first on line to buy it...?

BOTTOM LINE ACTION STEP:

Engage your customers by creating a survey to improve your products and services.

MINE YOUR *Own* BUSINESS

Your best prospects for new business and charitable donations may be right under your thumb. In fact, they are probably grouped amongst your existing clients and donors. A few tips on how to "mine" your customer base to enhance your business and ensure customer loyalty.

"Walmart is coming!" While this pronouncement may send a shudder down the spines of retailers within the local community that a Walmart location is being planning, we can all certainly learn how to increase our business from America's most successful retailer.

Walmart is a pioneer in the use of "data mining." Mining for data is similar to mining for gold, because the finds can be highly rewarding. It differs in that instead of requiring backbreaking labor with heavy equipment, data mining can be done with a few well-placed key strokes on our computers. Data mining allows us to unlock valuable information contained within our own databases and customer files, helping us do more business with existing customers, and making them happier for doing that business with us.

We don't even have to spend the millions that Walmart does, or even use all of their sophisticated techniques. You may already have the software you need in your existing database. In fact, in many cases, by studying individual invoices, you should be able to detect purchasing patterns.

Why is this so vital to your business's growth?

You probably have customers with seasonal needs who place orders at certain times of the year. Data mining can make this information handier, so that you can time a special offer in advance of their next anticipated purchase. Same goes for donors in the world of fundraising. People tend to donate on birthdays or other important momentous occasions in their lives. Scheduling periodic reviews of your records will aid you immeasurably in finding new opportunities with your existing clients.

This brings us to one of the most important but overlooked topics in marketing. Segmentation.

One major advantage of segmentation is that it provides you with an analysis of your existing customers and categorizes them by groups. For example, if you are a financial advisor, you will want to group your clients by investment category. So, when you see a company whose shares are poised to rise, or that AAA insured tax-free bond that will allow your customers to sleep at night; time is then of the essence before the deal disappears. You will know exactly whom to call and what to offer.

If you are a store owner, ideally, you would like to track the items that customers tend to buy in the same visit. Here too, we can look up to Walmart, who upon reviewing sales slips, found that male shoppers were showing up on Thursday nights to buy their weekend supplies of beer and diapers. They wisely moved these two items to adjacent displays.

Baltimore-based marketing analyst EJ Barry has some really powerful ideas on segmentation. You won't find the following line in the Bill of Rights, but EJ Barry says it without mincing words. "Segmentation is based on the precept that not all customers are equal. Some can't live without your product; others couldn't care less. Some customers are highly profitable; others are only marginally profitable or even cost you money."

Segmentation helps you identify potential based on recurring patterns. After all, history repeats itself. All businesses have seen marginal customers whose orders suddenly grew exponentially. There were probably some signs in advance that could have tipped this off. Wouldn't it be nice to be aware of such "buy" signals to woo similar customers who display those same attributes? By the same token, customers who may be in the process of dropping a vendor, normally display warning signs. If we grouped those warning signs, and stayed alert for them, we might be able to prevent the loss of a good customer, or even nudge a troublesome or unprofitable one elsewhere.

Any time is an opportune time to mine our own businesses and dig up as many informational nuggets as possible. Sounds like it's time to consult with a professional marketing firm who can advise your company on how to dig up the date – and more importantly – use the valuable data to grow your business.

BOTTOM LINE ACTION STEP:
Get to know your data and you'll get to know your customers.

CUTTING *the* MUSTARD

Every company would like their product or brand name to become and remain a household word. To succeed, one needs some ingenuity and a long-range plan, but the ultimate rewards are more than worthwhile.

Many folks are deliriously happy when the annual Nathan's Famous Annual International Hot Dog Eating contest gets underway, especially the makers of Rolaids and Maalox, whose antacid products are needed in copious quantities by participants who down as many as 60 or more hot dogs in ten minutes. Ugghh!! Many others are elated, if not inflated, when the contest is over and the coveted "Mustard Belt" and grand prize of around $10,000 has been awarded to the winner (who hopes that it will cover his gastroenterologist's bill).

This annual contest that Nathan's has cooked up has become part of America's July 4th ritual, along with apple pie, fireworks and doubleheaders. To whet people's appetites, Nathan's Famous erected a huge electronic scoreboard at the contest site in Coney Island, which they call the Wall of Fame. It shows pictures of previous contest winners and, most importantly from a publicist's point of view, a countdown clock with blinking red LED numbers showing how many days, hours, minutes and seconds until the next contest begins. What Nathan's scoreboard boils down to is a year-long advertising and promotional campaign for a competition that lasts all of 10 or 12 minutes.

Is it worth it?

If you were to grill me about this, I would tell you that a small part of me can relate to those who bellyache and feel that the surrounding publicity is overdone, which is a terrible thing to do to a hot dog.

While I'm not advocating for the product itself, from a marketing point of view, Nathan's concept has a lot of beef to it. People have to eat three times a day. There are tens of thousands of food products from which to choose and even when a person decides to eat out, there are endless choices. How do you get people to keep your fare topmost in their minds? Nathan's figured out they had to do something, even something wacky, to keep their name at the top of the menu.

It really works for them. A recent click on Nathan's on Google Finance displayed their top ten news stories. Seven of those ten were either about this upcoming contest or other smaller ones the company sponsors nationwide. Today, Nathan's has expanded to become an international fast food chain with a market value of nearly $100 million. That's not bad for a company that started with one stand in Coney Island in 1916 where they sold hot dogs for a nickel. That's probably what a parking fine cost back then in case you got nabbed double-parking along the boardwalk. (Yes, they had cars back then too – a Ford Model T cost about $360!)

There is also a method to Nathan's madness. Their campaign accomplishes much more than what appears at face value. The Wendover Group in England recently conducted a study on customer retention during difficult economic times. They say that in most industries, customer attrition can be anywhere between 10% and 40% in any single year. Losing a customer is costly in more ways than one. Besides the lost revenue, you have to find a new customer and Wendover analysts say replacing a customer is typically five to ten times more expensive than keeping existing ones.

One way to retain customers is to keep your name out there. Of course nothing makes a company into a top dog more than a good product at a fair price plus great service. Yet, we can all learn from Nathan's that if you want to keep your name at the tips of customer's tongues, you first have to position it constantly in their minds (and in this case, their bellies).

BOTTOM LINE ACTION STEP:

Come up with creative ways to stay on your customer's minds.

STRATEGIC PLANNING

“ *By failing to prepare
you are preparing to fail.* ”
— *Benjamin Franklin*

IMAGINE THIS...

Imagine you're boarding an airplane to embark on an international flight.

You navigate down the narrow aisle, manhandle your oversized carry-on into the undersized luggage compartment, and squeeze into seat 27F – all while being serenaded with the crackling symphony of passengers munching on their complimentary salted peanuts. Sounds typical, right?

The pilot turns on the static-prone PA system and begins with the traditional pre-flight announcement:

"Ladies and gentleman, this is your Captain speaking. Welcome aboard Flight 909 and we hope you enjoy the flight. If you take a look out the side windows, you will observe that our airplane has no wings – but please, there's no need to panic!

"While our tight budget didn't allow for wings to be installed, you can be assured that this aircraft is in the hands of a most experienced flight crew. We are sure that the crew can make this journey happen, despite our lack of wings. Thank you and have a nice flight."

The deathly silence following this strange announcement would be immediately punctuated by shrieking passengers making a mad dash for the nearest exit, and a few hapless souls left choking on their salted peanuts.

You're probably thinking that this story is supposed to be some sort of joke. But believe it or not, it's actually an everyday occurrence. Oh no, I'm not referring specifically to the airline industry – I am talking about the thousands of businesses and organizations that eliminate their marketing expenditures...and still expect profits to soar upwards into the sky.

You can be the greatest pilot in the world; the best businessman in the universe; or have the most amazing company in the galaxy. But without the thrust of marketing's wings, your corporate jet will never lift off the ground. In essence, marketing is to a business what wings are to an airplane.

This important, but often neglected point was highlighted in a recent news story titled, "Out of sight is out of business." According to Reuters World News, a study performed by Nielson IAG (a marketing research and polling company), showed that consumer confidence in a company or business is dramatically influenced by the company's advertising and marketing efforts.

In the study, over 55% of those who had seen multiple ads from prominent banking institutions over a six month span, possessed a high level of trust and confidence with the institution.

Alternatively, only 18% of adults had confidence in a prominent banking institution of which they saw little or no advertising (see Figure A).

"This research shows that companies who remain out of sight can actually end up out of business," said Richard E. Khaleel, Vice President of Nielson IAG Financial Services. As illustrated by this study, advertising and marketing efforts play a crucial role in a business's success – or failure.

Case in point: In the beginning of 2008 (before the financial crisis erupted), certain financial services companies began cutting back on ad spending. And guess what? These companies ended their quarter with revenues down by over 13%. Surprised? We're not.

Often, companies slash their advertising budgets with the misguided justification of saving money. And just as often, this is followed with a drastic decrease in sales and plunging profits.

During the Great Depression, cereal manufacturer Kellogg's doubled their advertising budget at a time when their main competitor was cutting back on advertising. The consequences of their actions were quite clear: "By 1933, even as the economy cratered, Kellogg's profits had risen almost thirty percent and it has become what it remains today: the industry's dominant player," writes James Surowiecki, in the financial page of The New Yorker.

But that's not all.

The Reuters article quoted above stressed that businesses utilizing an array of advertising, direct-mail, email, and electronic media gained higher profits, than those that didn't. In fact, one of the biggest profit-generators came from marketing efforts launched in large newspapers. Oh, and about that earlier airplane story?

214

Don't let it scare you. Current FAA guidelines require that all airplanes be equipped with wings – but maybe not peanuts!

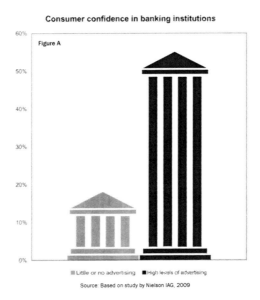

Consumer confidence in banking institutions

Figure A

Little or no advertising   High levels of advertising

Source: Based on study by Nielson IAG, 2009

BOTTOM LINE ACTION PLAN:

Out of the customer's sight could mean out of business for you.
Always keep your eye on the future.

IS THE GLASS HALF FULL *or* HALF EMPTY?

Is the glass half full or half empty? This age-old question has been debated by optimists and pessimists since time immemorial. While their verdict has yet to be decided, those in the advertising and marketing industry have solved this riddle long ago: The glass is unequivocally, absolutely, undisputedly half-full. And boy is it ever!

While pessimists may have a hard time believing it, times of adversity are also great harbingers of opportunity.

According to an article published in The New York Times ("Is it a recession? Marketers seem to think so!"), businesses of all sizes aggressively pounce on the beneficial advertising, marketing and positioning opportunities offered by a recession. In fact, behemoth retailer Walmart built up a new advertising approach based solely on saving money – a lucrative sales pitch sure to attract customers floundering in the midst of an economic crisis. "Save money. Live better," was their slogan, revamped during a recession period.

But, while this marketing slogan and the positioning behind it sounds fine and dandy, does it actually work? "Amidst widespread consumer anxiety, Walmart weathered a difficult holiday season for retailers, reporting a 2.7 percent increase for December, while many rivals, including Target, posted losses," wrote Times reporter Stuart Elliott in the article. In other words, the answer to the aforementioned question is a resounding, reverberating, cash-register ringing...yes!

And while many businesses use an economic crisis to beef up their advertising messages, just as many harness an economy's sorry status as an advertising message itself. According to The Times, North Fork Bank – now Capital One – launched advertisements stating: "Uncertain times call for a very certain rate," as a pitch for their low, fixed-rate bond certificates.

Instead of focusing on aesthetics or performance, Nissan highlighted the gas-saving, spend-less-at-the-pump virtues of its new Nissan Altima sedan.

In all, while strategic-based marketing may be a costly investment, shunning the benefits offered by advertising and marketing can prove far more costly. Smart companies and businesses owners always use trying economic times to their benefit – and so should you!

Now that we've addressed the importance of advertising and marketing during a recession, I will touch upon a related question that people ask all the time: Why does advertising during rough economic times significantly boost profits? After all, logic dictates that companies cutting back on costly advertising should be the ones left with more money, compared to their spending-big-money-on-advertising competition. But as we've illustrated above, the reality shows otherwise. What gives?

While there are many ways of approaching this, the most common and logical answer is as follows: When everybody is flooding the media channels with advertising for their products, services, companies and organizations, it's harder for your business to stand out. It's difficult to distinguish your ad from the many on the pages before and after your ad; before and after your radio commercial; before and after your web banner... well, you get the point.

When ads are scarcer however, your advertising's success factor rises simply because you have more face-time with potential consumers than the non-advertising competition does. Interestingly enough, according to a Bain & Company (a global business and strategy consulting firm) study, twice as many companies soared from the bottom of their industries to the top during the recession of 1990 and 1991, possibly due to this reasoning.

A similar, metaphorical reason for this effect can be attributed to the doom sayers and so-called financial gurus who thrive on reporting negative hype about the economy. This can be explained with the story of a Manhattan hot dog vendor whose business grew tremendously through aggressive marketing. When the vendor's friend (a so-called financial guru) told him that a great recession was coming, the man nervously took down his sign and didn't market his products anymore. His sales plunged, and he concluded that his so-called financial guru buddy was right – a recession had arrived!

The hot dog vendor's competition though, was told by a good friend (a smart businessman who owned successful companies) that an opportunity for boosting sales was arriving. He enthusiastically enlarged his sign, increased his marketing efforts and brought in more profits than ever before!

The bottom line? Let's not take our cue from the story's first hot dog vendor and his pessimistic friend, but rather let us learn from the sensible ways of the second vendor. Through foresight, planning and smart marketing, you too can successfully grow your business and bottom line (no pun intended)!

BOTTOM LINE ACTION STEP:

Use trying economic times to your benefit and market yourself to grow in good times and in bad.

LEARNING *from* NASA...

Several years ago, NASA sent the shuttle Atlantis on a space mission to repair the aging Hubble Telescope.

While NASA's engineers and astronauts had trained extensively for this mission and anticipated a simple spacewalk repair, unexpected problems kept cropping up. At one point, Astronaut Michael Massimino – while floating 350 miles above Earth – had to put aside his expensive power tools and resort to brute force, breaking away a jammed bolt attached to a rail on the telescope, setting the mission behind schedule.

"NASA, which prides itself on being prepared, had not anticipated a bolt problem while removing the foot-and-a-half-long handrail," said lead flight controller Tony Ceccacci, according to an Associated Press news release.

While some viewed this as yet another news story, I saw a major lesson that applies to marketing and business in general. Think about it – NASA, the space exploration program renowned for its methodological planning and preparation abilities, was caught completely off guard by a simple metal bolt!

220

You don't have to be a rocket scientist to appreciate the irony of this. If you are in the world of business, it may sound rather familiar. Sometimes, despite the best research, groundwork and preparation, marketing campaigns don't always go according to plan. It can be as a result of many underlying factors, both internal and external.

That's why it is crucial to closely monitor the ongoing results of a marketing campaign and make adjustments when necessary. Sometimes the adjustments may consist of a simple tweak. Other times it can be in the form of a good yank that wasn't initially part of the plan. But being open to adapting to a situation is key to an effective marketing plan.

Remember the **"Four P's"** (**P**roduct, **P**ricing, **P**lacement and **P**romotion)? Although planning from the outset is critical, when necessary, the Four P's may need to be adjusted as you roll out your marketing campaign. The Harvard professor that developed the **"Four P's"** concept understood that marketing is not a rigid set of rules; rather, it is a mixture of flexible components that can be tweaked as needed.

A great example – in product development – was when a scientist at innovation company 3M, developed a weak adhesive that didn't stick well. At first, it was thought to be useless – until a colleague came up with the idea of applying it to small yellow papers and using them as temporary bookmarks. The result? Those sticky little Post-It notes that adorn/clutter your desk, books, computer monitor, office walls, and even the refrigerator! By adapting to the situation, 3M was able to market what was thought to be a worthless product... and transform it into a multi-million dollar idea.

How about this one? When inventor James Wright came up with a gooey-like substance while trying to find an alternative to rubber, he didn't think much of it and let it languish in his laboratory for several years. However, when it fell into the hands of marketing consultant Peter Hodgson, it was instantly transformed from an odd invention into a profitable toy – Silly Putty!

And the next time you enjoy a refreshing Popsicle on a hot summer day, be sure to thank the marketing ingenuity of eleven-year-old Frank Epperson. In 1905, young Frank stirred together a mixture of soda powder and water, and accidently left it on his cold porch. The next day, Frank went to retrieve his drink... and was in for a surprise.

The wooden stirrer inside the cup had frozen together with the sweet mixture. Instead of throwing it out, he decided to eat the delicious-tasting frozen mixture by holding onto the attached wooden stick. A few years later, Frank applied for a patent and began to market this frozen anomaly as a refreshing summer treat. And the rest, as they say, is Popsicle history.

So, Popsicle aficionados and businessmen unite – and keep in mind how the benefits of marketing can significantly sweeten your business!

BOTTOM LINE ACTION STEP:
While planning is key to a marketing plan and to a business, remain open and flexible to adapt it to changing situations.

7 PROVEN WAYS _to_ BEAT A RECESSION

Let's face it: recessions impact everyone – individuals, families, governments and businesses.

Everyone tightens their belt in a recession and with cost cutting measures being put in place, many businesses have been forced to cut back on their advertising and marketing expenditures, leading to lost sales and diminishing profits.

But take heart. While that may seem depressing (especially if you are in the midst of a recession), it's actually about to turn quite positive. You see, my point is not to emphasize all the gloom and doom, but rather focus on the proverbial silver lining that can be applied to your businesses' marketing efforts – at little or no cost.

In the midst of any turbulent economy or even a recession, it is imperative that business owners overcome the panic and paralysis that have gripped many companies and businesses – and launch effective marketing techniques to help combat this problem.

Distinguished marketing personality and close friend, Yosi Heber, former Senior Marketing Executive at Kraft and Dannon, and now President of Oxford Hill Partners, LLC, wrote an article for the prestigious Advertising Age magazine on this topic. I am basing the following points on this article and I want to thank him for allowing me to enlighten you with his valuable insights:

1. Firstly, companies and businesses can combat the effects of any recession by creating a marketing strategy based on current economic conditions and focusing on promoting their core business message.

    For example, Kraft Foods' DiGiorno Pizza created an effective advertising campaign emphasizing that a delivered pizza costs $16.13 while a DiGiorno pizza costs only $6.69. And its clever tag line brings that point home – "DiGiorno: Fresh delivery taste without the delivery price". Simply put, the Kraft campaign clearly highlights the quality and value their product offers. Nothing too cheesy here (besides the Mozzarella) – just a balanced marketing strategy targeted at a wobbly economy.

2. Remember the detective board game, Clue, which you played as a youngster? Well, your sleuthing days are far from over. Those valuable deducing and problem-solving skills will help you win more than just the game – they'll help you win more business.

    Be sure to keep tabs on other businesses, organizations and companies within your industry. Monitor their pricing strategies, advertising and positioning angles. Regularly review their websites, press releases and press coverage to learn about their new products, promotions and strategic moves. The goal here is not to copy and imitate others; rather, it's to know what you're up against and how you can successfully differentiate yourself from the competition.

3. An ounce of prevention is worth a pound of cure, goes the old saying. Alternatively, when it comes to business and marketing, an ounce of prevention is worth a pound of Benjamin Franklins.

   Determine whether your company is prepared for a disaster and can act quickly on it. No, I'm not necessarily referring to floods or tornados; I am talking about your corporate landscape. What happens if your biggest client who accounts for 20% of your revenue goes bankrupt? Or if your largest distributor tosses your product line out with hardly an "Adiós." Or if your biggest donor is, unfortunately, no longer your biggest donor. Figure out what would happen to your bottom line in such a scenario and what your backup plan would be to mitigate the negative – and costly – effects.

4. Make sure your customers remain your customers. Enhance existing customer relationships to keep them coming back – and prevent them from going elsewhere.

   Lose your best customers, and you could be out of business. Send them relevant mailings and e-mails that inform, incentivize and entertain. Johnson & Johnson's BabyCenter does a great job with this. When a mother signs up, she gets relevant communications (based on her baby's age) customized with tips, tools and subtle promotions for Johnson & Johnson products. A loyalty program can also be a very powerful – and profitable – marketing tool.

5. Give customers a good reason to open their checkbooks. Incentives come in many shapes, forms and sizes – use them!

   Provide coupons, trial samples and free offers to give consumers an incentive to purchase your products, use your company or support your organization. And actively cross-sell related products the way certain chain-bookstores point out related books bundled together at discounted prices. Another example: Home Depot always has little displays containing nails in the aisles of the lumber section. After all, if somebody's buying a dozen 2x4s, chances are he'll need some nails to hammer them up with, right?

6. Grab hold of new customers. I don't mean physically of course, but do shout out the many unique benefits offered by your entity – and have your existing clients join the fray by doing so as well.

    Flaunt customer testimonials and success stories in your ads, brochures and media methods. Tap into word-of-mouth and viral techniques. Procter & Gamble's Tide website enables users to send e-mails to as many as five friends and challenge them to a Tide game. Also, tough times like these may be unique moments to grab retail shelf space from competitors. As trends change, retailers often reassess and discard non-performing brands.

7. Sometimes, less is more. And when it comes to packaging, if your pushing a product targeted at value-conscious consumers, this concept is most certainly true. Primarily, because less expensive packaging translates into lower cost margins, which translates into more sales, which translates into higher profits. That wasn't too complicated, was it?

    Remove unnecessary costs from your product or package to lower prices without hurting your margins. Cost-conscious consumers are often willing to get less – if they can pay less. Unilever's Skippy jar now has a dimple at the bottom. As a result, there is about 10% less peanut butter in the jar than before (16.3 ounces vs. 18 ounces). But customers keep on buying it, because as we all know, pricing is about more than just peanuts (no pun intended).

The bottom line? Marketing has many useful attributes that can build up a business before a recession; keep it afloat during a recession; and help it rebound after a recession.

So keep on tweaking and examining your marketing strategies from all angles. Don't be afraid to flaunt your company's attributes and highlight the customers who have benefitted from it. And last, but certainly not least, be sure to gain from and utilize the many benefits that marketing has to offer – to successfully keep your profits up in a down economy.

BOTTOM LINE ACTION STEP:

Don't give up when economic times are bad. Prepare a marketing plan to help get through a recession and prosper after.

FAILURE IS _not_ AN OPTION!

For those old enough to remember things such as record players, telegrams and rotary telephones, the story of Apollo 13 will probably ring a bell.

In April of 1970, three American astronauts were launched into space aboard a rocket ship called Apollo 13. Midway through the mission (and approximately 200,000 miles away from Planet Earth), an accidental explosion on board left the astronauts with almost no electrical power, water or oxygen. Many NASA scientists gloomily predicted that there was nothing to be done – the astronauts would meet their untimely end and be stranded in space forever.

They did not, however, take the determination and resolve of NASA's flight director, Gene Kranz, into account. Shortly after the explosion, Kranz gathered a team of engineers and scientists into a conference room and instructed them to cast aside their doubts about whether or not the astronauts could make it back alive. "The men aboard that spacecraft are going to make it back," he told them. "And you're all going to figure out how. *Because failure is not an option!*" With those powerful words, Gene Kranz inspired his team to rectify the problem and safely return Apollo 13 to Earth.

For those in the non-profit sector, Gene Kranz's significant words take on a meaning of their own: *"Failure is most certainly not an option!"*

In turbulent economic times, many businesses and organizations struggle to stay afloat. The never-ending landslide of rising expenses and shrinking revenues or donations can provide businesses, fund raisers and executive directors an excuse to "throw in the proverbial towel." But for dedicated individuals, *failure is not an option!*

For non-profits in particular, whether it's relationship fundraising, technical fundraising, event-driven fundraising, online fundraising, etcetera, the unwavering efforts undertaken by our non-profits are truly exemplary. They can – and should – serve as a source of inspiration to all of us in the business world as well.

Indeed, failure is not an option!

I recall reading an interesting story in an industry publication about how a donor who was an avid coin collector called two different non-profits with the following proposition: if they would have a penny drive (i.e. encouraging people to donate pennies), he would buy all the pennies from them (with the hopes that a few of them would be antiques) and match the grand total with a check of his own.

The first organization politely turned down the offer saying that it would be complicated and probably end up as a failure.

The second organization realized that a unique fundraiser such as a Penny-thon would not only generate revenue but presumably create major publicity as well, effectively getting their message out via multiple media sources! They pushed aside their doubts and tackled the challenge head-on with enthusiasm and gusto. As you can imagine, they made thousands of dollars in donations, widened their donor base significantly and the story landed as an article in many newspapers and magazines.

BOTTOM LINE ACTION STEP:

Capitalize on unique opportunities for the future. Avoid failure by seizing these opportunities.

TURNING OVER
A NEW LEAF

Even in a bad economy, someone with an entrepreneurial mind-set usually always has optimism for the future, optimism that there is opportunity around the corner. The entrepreneur usually is always looking ahead. Here are some creative ideas to get you into that entrepreneurial mind frame and get your business in shape for the future.

We often talk about year-end planning but to me, that's a misnomer. I prefer to use the term year-ahead planning. After all, jet planes don't have rear-view mirrors and if we want to prepare our businesses for take-off, we need to have a flight plan and know where we want to land.

It is easy to become over-absorbed in the day-to-day activities of running our businesses and overlook planning for the future. That would be a shame. I really appreciate the way Crain's New York Business phrased it: "things are often better than they look, and if looked at optimistically, we can grow."

I agree with a statement made by Scott Albro, founder and chief executive of Focus Inc. Scott said, "Small business owners should take ownership of the things they *can* control."

One area within your grasp is to reach out to colleagues, customers and suppliers, or to other people with an interest in your business and invite them to join your company's board of directors. This can be a far more valuable step than just plain networking. While networking is important, sometimes we tend to shake a lot of hands and share short introductions and snippets of conversation while looking around to see who else is in attendance that we might want to talk to. By establishing, or expanding a board, you are pooling talent and experience in an organized fashion with people who want to see you succeed. Having strategic partners, literally on-board, can provide you with new sources of valuable information and insight.

As your business expands, you are likely, at some point, to face hiring decisions. Before taking on new fixed costs, it pays to consider tapping into the burgeoning freelance market. This works especially well for seasonal businesses, and in general, it affords you with the opportunity to test how well the worker fits in and how much they can contribute, before making a full-time commitment.

Finally, remember to leverage your time appropriately. My good friend and noted business financial advisor, Jonathan Gassman CAP, CFP, CPA, is always pounding the table about Strategic Coach – a training course for entrepreneurs – which teaches business owners how to "multiply" themselves. While we can't (yet!) clone ourselves to be in two places or do two things at once, we can however implement time-saving technologies, utilize effective teamwork and delegate tasks to free ourselves to grow our businesses.

There's no such thing anymore as business as usual. If we view hard times we have experienced as an opportunity to step in and provide the products, services, and experiences that clients really want, then the future years will be our best ever.

BOTTOM LINE ACTION STEP:
Think like an entrepreneur and plan ahead for the future.

LESSONS *from* A RENOVATED BATHROOM

One of my friends recently decided to fix up his bathroom and asked me to come over and help him paint the walls. I figured painting would be fun — at least it was in kindergarten — and back then we got in trouble if we painted on the walls. Here was my opportunity, so I readily agreed and showed up bright and early.

And it was then and there in the bathroom that I learned a great lesson. Do it yourself home improvement projects and the marketing industry have a great deal in common – (or at least they should) — the need for proper planning. Think about it. A room can be painted only if you have the proper materials, a well researched plan, and the time to finish the project.

This lesson was hammered home when we ran out of paint halfway through. While purchasing more, we were told that bathrooms need a different type of paint, and by the time we purchased the correct paint and got home, it was too late in the day for us to finish the job. (After two weeks, his wife called in a painter.)

233

Likewise, a successful marketing campaign can only be launched if the company behind it sets aside time to analyze its target market, plan on how to project its message and utilize the proper marketing methods to execute the campaign. A marketing team that doesn't perform the proper research, planning and legwork will be throwing their time (and marketing dollars!) out the window.

To illustrate the importance of planning a successful marketing campaign or event, let's focus on a story involving a product that often ends up quenching our thirst after working up a sweat painting — Snapple.

The manufacturer of that tasty iced tea (peach is my favorite!) decided to launch a unique marketing campaign to highlight their newest product, Snapple popsicles. One way to market this product would be by attempting to make the largest frozen popsicle in world history; a feat that would land Snapple in the Guinness Book of World Records and generate tremendous media coverage and exposure.

But alas, the marketing whizzes behind this seemingly-clever summertime marketing ruse neglected to plan it all the way through.

According to an article published by The Associated Press (June 22, 2005), Snapple had been trying to promote a new line of frozen treats by setting a record for the world's largest popsicle, but called off the stunt before it was lifted fully upright by a construction crane. Authorities said they were worried the thing would collapse in the 80-degree, first-day-of-summer heat.

The 25-foot-tall, 17½-ton treat of frozen Snapple juice melted faster than expected, flooding Union Square in downtown Manhattan with kiwi-strawberry-flavored fluid that sent pedestrians scurrying for higher ground. The New York Fire Department was called and firefighters closed off several streets and used hoses to wash away the sugary goo.

While the above marketing ploy was undoubtedly clever, the logistics involved should have been planned properly to avoid transforming a good idea into a marketing fiasco.

Likewise, in April of 2001, computer giant IBM launched an off-beat marketing campaign that involved spray-painting the sidewalks of San Francisco's streets to promote its products. And it most certainly grabbed lots of attention – including the attention of the San Francisco City Council who slapped IBM with fines of over $120,000 in public property damages.

Because the bottom line is, no matter how brilliant, clever or creative it is, a marketing campaign will only be as good (and successful) as the planning and thought that goes into it.

BOTTOM LINE ACTION STEP:

Before undertaking any marketing initiative, do your research and plan ahead. Otherwise, you may be wasting money, time and resources.

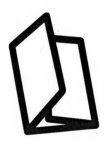

BROCHURES HELP YOU CLOSE THE DEAL
(make sure you have them in time)

Did you ever find yourself being asked in the middle of a presentation if you have anything in writing? Or did you ever attempt to sell a refrigerator or an electronic gadget, when the customer asked if you have a brochure with the specifications?

To put the questions raised above into context, from experience I've learned that anything that's put into writing and if it's presented attractively, should be impressive enough to greatly assist in closing any deal.

This same principle applies to non-profit organizations. The concern that a surly donor may quip, "if you can afford such a fancy brochure, why do you need my donation?" can be easily answered. Without getting into the specifics, in most cases, the one that answers with that quip, is just validating his or her conscience not to contribute to your cause. (You can verify that by checking that 'prospective donor's' past giving habits). Secondly, even if they add that off-the-cuff remark, after they go through your brochure, they definitely know more about your cause than they did before you handed them the brochure!

Non-profits must, and do spend on publicity and marketing. The American Institute of Philanthropy's Charity Rating Guide (AIP) gives satisfactory grades to organizations that allocate as much as 40% of their budgets to fundraising and administration, and it rates as "highly efficient" those who spend up to 25% for such costs. The AIP warns donors about organizations who advertise that their costs of fundraising are zero.

Serious donors are usually successful businesspeople who know that you must invest before you begin to earn. They expect something in writing. They want to "kick the tires" and see the specs of your organization, which in the case of a non-profit, includes your mission statement, your significant accomplishments to date, your goals (... and don't forget, lots of photos!)

Having established the need for written materials, the challenge turns to focusing your message. Non-profits generally require brochures for recruitment, fundraising, or raising awareness. Sometimes they need one of each because it is critical not to send out mixed signals. If your goal is to persuade parents to enroll their children in your private school, don't ask for a donation at the same time. (The tuition is tough enough to come up with!) If the goal is to raise money for a building campaign, your message must be aimed squarely at enthusing donors. You need to show them the end result of their donation – for you and for them.

There is one common denominator, however, no matter what the brochure type. You must show the reader what you do, rather than what you are. In sales, we describe this approach in terms of features and benefits. The fact that the newest Maytag refrigerator has a 25-cubic foot capacity is a feature. The idea that it has enough shelf space inside so that you can actually see and easily find everything you stuffed inside (and still have additional room left over to store those midnight snacks) is the benefit.

The challenge, in a recruitment brochure for example, is to demonstrate to parents how your methods of teaching and your facilities will be conducive to a proper and enriching education. In a brochure for a private boarding school, we formulated the tagline "preparing for the future" and a page header "home away from home." The latter opened the door to describe the school's extensive dormitory modernization to assure parents that their children would be safe and comfortable.

We now understand why we need brochures and a few guidelines on how to craft them. Last but not least is the timing. In the outstanding 2004 book *Strategic Planning for Public Relations*, now in its third edition, author Ronald D. Smith says it takes an average of 41 days from initial planning until you actually get your brochures to the post office (not to mention how long it may take for the post office to deliver them).

Time flies. Yesterday would have been the best time to start brainstorming on how to make an effective brochure, but today is not too late!

BOTTOM LINE ACTION STEP:

Don't wait for the last minute. Get the word out about your next major event, fundraising or recruitment drive for the world's most important organization — your own.

FOCUS DAY: HERE TO STAY

Revenue-generating activities comprise the lifeblood of any business. Revenue-generators include calling on and meeting current and prospective clients, marketing, advertising, and networking. However, we often allow any number of distractions to draw us away from these truly vital tasks. That's why we must learn to discipline ourselves to truly sharpen our focus.

Americans have always placed a premium on how to secure our retirement years financially, but in order to get to the stage where we can kick back and live comfortably, we normally have to put in 40 to 50 years of hard work.

Harrowing as that may sound, if you configure your schedule properly, your hard labor can be rewarded handsomely. Much however depends on how you allocate your time.

In 2013, I called a 'timeout' to join the Strategic Coach Program, founded by Dan Sullivan. Dan bills himself as the "world's foremost expert on entrepreneurship in action." After attending a few Strategic Coach workshops, I can attest to the fact that the program lives up to his billing.

I've had the opportunity to meet with Dan personally. Besides being impressed by his business brilliance, I can vouch for his ability to unleash an executive's innate drive. (Special shout-out to Marc Bodner, Jonathan Gassman and David Schild who all strongly recommended that I join the program). The courses have boosted my abilities to serve my loyal clients, inspire my team members and as a result, grow my business.

Much of the information that the workshops offer are confidential to those who are enrolled for the courses, so I can't go into extensive detail, but I can share a fundamental lesson that is instilled: the importance of structuring our workweek.

Under Strategic Coach's time system, The Entrepreneurial Time System, each day needs to be categorized in one of 3 ways: **1) Focus Day 2) Buffer Day or 3) Free Day.**

Free Days mean that you are off, totally. No stepping into the office, no working from home and no emails! As an Orthodox Jew, I'm fortunate that I have a natural advantage of more than 60 free days – in the form of the Sabbath and Festivals – built into each year where we are prohibited from doing any kind of labor and liberated from the bonds of our hi-tech contraptions.

Buffer Days are for chores than are necessary to maintain our businesses but don't directly generate revenue.

I want to focus on **Focus Days.** It's a subject that any executive who wants to expand their strategic vision, or grow their business in a measurable way should take to heart.

On Focus Days, we devote our time *exclusively* to activities that bring money into the business. Of course, this varies from business to business, but under their system, you first have to quantify your top three money-making activities. He instructs us to review our revenue figures – specifically how much we have earned on our best days. Using that figure as a benchmark, you set goals for how much revenue you would like your business to generate in the next 90 days, and then calculate how many Focus Days you need in the next three months to hit that goal.

To get the most out of a Focus Day, you have to fill that day's calendar in advance. Which means that before you leave the office prior to a focus day, you need to completely map the day out. What time are you going to get in the office or hop in your car to make that first sales call? Who are you going to meet with? What business proposition are you going to discuss? Have the Focus Day set up, literally hour by hour.

To leverage Focus Days to your ultimate advantage, spend some time – on Buffer Days – to analyze your best revenue-generating activities so that you know what's working, and what's not. Once you have that down pat, you can find ways of improving those activities and implementing them at peak efficiency.

You can be at your productive best if you set aside Focus Days and concentrate 100% of your efforts on activities that generate revenues and block out all distractions. Just say no to any extraneous phone calls or emails and don't engage in any activity that isn't focused on revenues.

BOTTOM LINE ACTION STEP:
Plan and prepare for truly productive focus days.